# Strategic Organization Design

## Concepts, Tools, & Processes

# Strategic Organization Design

## Concepts, Tools, & Processes

**David Nadler**
Delta Consulting Group

**Michael Tushman**
Columbia University

Scott, Foresman and Company
Glenview, Illinois     London, England

**Library of Congress Cataloging-in-Publication Data**

Nadler, David.
   Strategic organization design.

   Includes indexes.
   1. Organizational behavior.    2. Organization.
I. Tushman, Michael.    II. Title.
HD58.7.N33 1988    658.4'012    87-9832
ISBN 0-673-15860-8

1 2 3 4 5 6 – EBI – 92 91 90 89 88 87

# Foreword

The Management Applications Series is concerned with the application of contemporary research, theory, and techniques. There are many excellent books at advanced levels of knowledge, but few address the application of such knowledge. The authors in this series are uniquely qualified for this purpose, since they are all scholars who have experience in implementing change in real organizations through the methods they write about.

Each book treats a single topic in depth. When the choice is between presenting many approaches briefly or a single approach thoroughly, we have opted for the latter. Thus, after reading the book, the student or practitioner should know how to apply the methodology described.

Selection of topics for the series was guided by contemporary relevance to management practice, and by the availability of an author qualified as an expert yet able to write at a basic level of understanding. No attempt is made to cover all management methods, nor is any sequence implied in the series, although the books do complement one another. For example, change methods might fit well with managing by objectives.

The books in this series may be used in several ways. They may be used to supplement textbooks in basic courses on management, organizational behavior, personnel, or industrial psychology/sociology. Students appreciate the fact that the material is immediately applicable. Practicing managers will want to use individual books to increase their skills, either through self-study or in connection with management development programs, inside or outside of the organization.

Alan C. Filley

# Preface

The primary objectives of this book are to simplify a vast, complex area of study and help people understand organizations and their design. Therefore, it is aimed at potential designers of organizations, including executives, managers, staff people, consultants, and students. It should also be helpful to people in organizations who are merely trying to make some sense of what is going on around them.

As a simple treatment of a complex subject, this book is not a survey of the field; it does not cover all perspectives and does not try to be objective about various approaches. This book reflects one approach that we have found to be useful in our own understanding of organizations. This approach also seems to work when we teach it to other people—they seem to understand it and report that they can use the tools we provide. We present concepts to help the designer understand the rationale for various designs and to help people make organization design decisions. We have drawn on a large body of research but have not filled the text with footnotes or references.

The origin of this book goes back to 1975, when we were charged with teaching a course on management and organizational behavior to incoming MBAs at the Graduate School of Business, Columbia University. We agreed that prospective managers should know something about organization design, but we could not find an integrated, useful, and pragmatic approach to teaching this topic. We therefore began to develop such an approach, drawing on our own research and on that of our colleagues, some of whom had been instrumental in our own development. As a consequence, we need to acknowledge many people. Some people who are not listed here may feel left out, and to them we apologize. Some people listed here may not want to be associated with our work; to them we wish to clarify that we alone take full responsibility for this book.

First, we want to thank those organizations that have helped us, either as clients or as sites for our research. Without these organizations we could never have put together these ideas and this book. The following organizations were particularly helpful because they provided us with an opportunity either to do major design experiments or to try our ideas by teaching their managers how to make design decisions: Mountain Bell, Citibank, Honeywell, and Union Carbide.

Second, we wish to thank some individuals who have worked intensively as our colleagues in the search for understanding organization design. From 1978 to 1981, Robert Maher, Manager of the Organizational Effectiveness Group at AT&T, worked with us to develop a practical, teachable approach to design. He was a great collaborator, and we are greatly in his debt. Similarly, William Buehler, currently Vice-President at AT&T, has provided opportunities to use our design approach in a number of settings over the years; we also extend our thanks to him. Our work on organization design has been encouraged by the GTE Corporation; in particular, Randy McDonald, Vice-President of Organization Development, and Bruce Carswell, Senior Vice-President, Human Resources and Administration, have been tremendously helpful in providing pragmatic tests of our ideas. We are greatly in their debt.

Third, we want to recognize some broad seminal influences. Both of us basically learned organization design from Paul Lawrence of the Harvard Business School. Paul turned on some lights for us, making us aware of some new and unique ways of thinking about organization design. We are proud to have had the honor of being his students and hope that this work reflects well on our teacher. We also have been greatly influenced by Jay Galbraith. We consider our efforts to be a complement to his, an extension of the approach that he pioneered. Through Paul and Jay we also owe a debt to the late James Thompson, who said many profound and insightful things in a small book on organizations in 1967.

Finally, we want to thank our colleagues at the Delta Consulting Group (formerly Organizational Research and Consultation Inc.) and at Columbia University. While everyone at Delta has had a hand in developing the design material, several people have had a more major role — Carl Hill and Bob Bonadies. Ron Dukenski and Dale Wheeler, formerly of OR&C, also provided assistance and good ideas during the early development of this material. At Columbia, Elaine Romanelli provided great insight, while Joel Brockner and William Newman provided valuable feedback and constructive criticism.

Our greatest hope is that students of and people in organizations will read this book, find it understandable, and use the concepts to help build better organizations. That is what it is all about.

D.A.N.
M.L.T.

# Contents

8    *A Process for Making Design Decisions*    122

9    *Strategic Linking and the Informal Organization:*
    *Managing Organization Cultures*    138

10    *Implementing New Designs:*
    *Managing Organizational Change*    161

# 1

# Organization Design as a Managerial Tool

This book is an attempt to develop a pragmatic approach to strategic organization design that reflects the substantial amount of existing research on design and effectiveness. The text focuses on **concepts** for thinking about organizations and organization design, **tools** that are useful in designing organizations, and specific **processes** for making strategic design decisions. Throughout the book case examples are used to illustrate the ideas. Each chapter begins with a short case that illustrates the issues to be covered.

**Case 1:**

Amity Bank Ltd., located in the capital city of the country of Sapong, is a wholly owned subsidiary of a large, multinational financial services organization. Amity is the fourth largest bank in Sapong and has long held a reputation for innovation and leadership.

The bank is organized into two basic units (see Figure 1-1), which are largely self-contained and serve different customer groups. The Consumer Banking Group contains a variety of businesses, each aimed at providing specific products or services to individual customers. The Institutional Banking Group provides banking services to large corporations, to other banks, and to other types of public and private organizations, although the bulk of the business is with corporations.

In the last two years, the Institutional Banking Group has suffered from intense competition. In particular, the increasing

FIGURE 1-1      Amity Bank, Sapong, Organization Chart

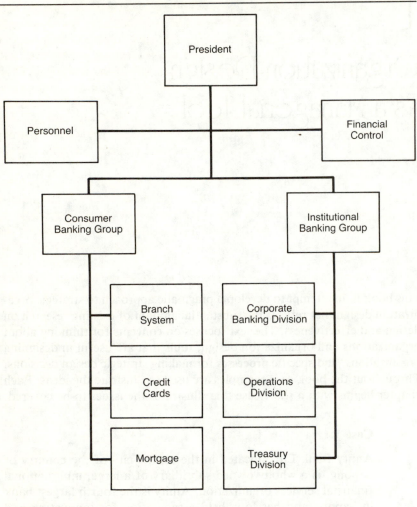

sophistication of corporate customers, combined with an influx of new foreign banks into the Sapong market, have decreased the "spreads" at Amity (the difference between the interest rate that Amity has to pay to get money and the rate it can charge its customers to whom it lends money). As a result, the profits in the Institutional Group have fallen significantly.

The Institutional Group is structured into three basic units. The Corporate Banking Division is made up largely of account managers, loan officers, credit analysts, and others involved in selling the bank's services to corporate customers. Primarily, they sell "credit," that is, they convince corporations to borrow money from and to place their cash deposits with Amity. The Operations Division is responsible for all of the processing, paperwork, and other "back office" functions in support of the Corporate Division's activities. The Treasury Division is largely made up of traders who buy and sell currency in the Sapong money market. Their primary role is to obtain money for the Corporate Division to lend, at as favorable a price as possible. In addition, Treasury does some trading of its own funds and executes foreign currency deals.

While the Institutional Group was experiencing profit pressures, the group's senior management also saw some unique opportunities because of Amity's parent company's investment in high technology (electronic banking) and locally because of the development of a strong Treasury Group that could perform well in various activities, such as foreign exchange transactions. After several months of discussion, the senior team of the Institutional Group came up with a new strategy that called for Amity to start aggressively offering packages of services that included both traditional loans and financing but which also included electronic and treasury services for a fee. They felt that the total package would give Amity something unique and enable the bank to charge customers more because of the "added value" that Amity would bring.

Six months after the announcement of the new strategy, the senior team met to assess progress. After several hours of discussion, they had to admit that things had not gone as planned. While the three divisions were supposed to be working together to assemble and sell packages of financial services, in reality there was a great deal of conflict among the divisions. Corporate bankers complained that their job was to bring in big deals, not "plug in terminals." The Treasury dealers complained that the Corporate people were making demands on them that conflicted with their own primary trading strategies. The Operations people, who felt that they now should be making calls on customers to discuss technology, felt that the Corporate account managers were snubbing them. In general, few new package deals were being executed, and people were primarily doing what they had been doing previously, except for spending more time in argumentative meetings with the other divisions. Although the senior team felt committed to the new strategy, they had to admit that it was not working.

**Case 2:**

Parkside Medical Center is a large, well-known organization with an international reputation for excellence in teaching and research. The medical center has two major operating units (see Figure 1-2): the medical school (charged with the primary responsibilities of teaching and research) and the 1000-bed Parkside Hospital (to deliver patient care and provide a setting for the research work of the medical school faculty). The medical school is divided by discipline into a number of academic departments. The faculty serve as staff to the hospital as well. The hospital is headed by a director to whom the major departments, including Nursing, Support Services, Clinical Services, and Social Services, report.

The department most closely associated with direct delivery of patient care is the Nursing Department. Five assistant directors report to the Director of Nursing, and each is responsible for a set of patient care units located in a particular hospital building. In turn, nursing supervisors report to each assistant director. Each nursing supervisor is responsible for a particular unit. The hospital grew through successive additions to the buildings, and, as a result, each building includes specialized units that care for a variety of patients. Thus, a building might have one surgery unit, three medical units, one pediatrics unit, and one orthopedic surgery unit. Similarly, surgery units might be spread out among three or four buildings. All of the clinical services (laboratories such as radiology, nuclear medicine, blood bank, and pharmacy) are centrally located and serve all patient care units. Similarly, all of the support services (the "hotel" services such as food, housekeeping, and transportation) are centrally run.

A major concern of the president of the medical center in recent years has been the quality of patient care. While Parkside is known for technical excellence, recently it has also become known as a bad place to be a patient. Patient surveys have painted a picture of the hospital as impersonal and cold, a place where patients do not receive courteous and responsive treatment from nurses and other on-unit personnel. Patients are constantly shuttled among various units and laboratories, rarely seeing the same staff over time. They report feeling as if they are being processed through a large factory.

During the past year, a task force has been looking at the quality of patient care. This task force examined all of the different experiments and projects aimed at improving patient care and found that not one had made a significant or sustained positive impact on patient care. The task force also noted that these

FIGURE 1-2    Parkside Medical Center Partial Organization Chart

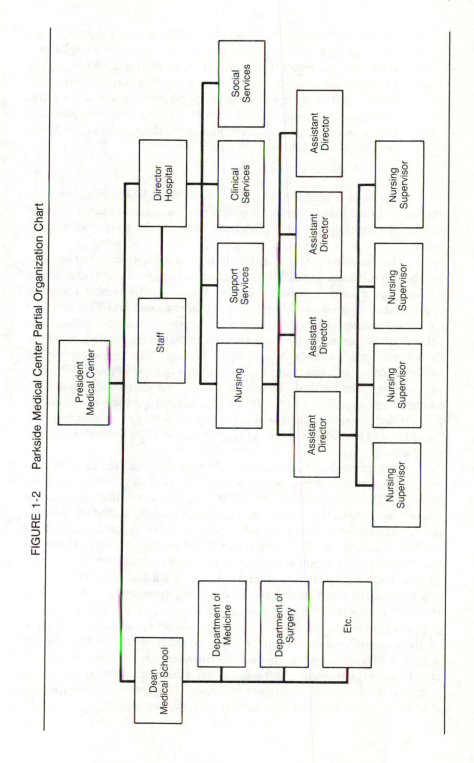

efforts seemed to suffer from an inability to find the proper unit or target level within the organization in order to bring about improvement. Every time a unit or set of units was identified, the project was hampered by a constantly changing cast of char-acters—different physicians, shifting patients, and rotating staff. The conclusion was that if a patient care improvement program or process were to work, a fundamental change in the hospital's organization would have to take place.

These two cases, Amity Bank and Parkside Hospital, provide examples of the kinds of problems with which managers are faced and that lead them to consider reshaping, restructuring, or redesigning their organi-zations.

In the case of Amity, a shift in the competitive environment has led the organization to rethink its business strategy and to create a new approach to providing services. The problem is that this new approach requires the three key units—Corporate, Operations, and Treasury—to closely coordinate their efforts in the development, shaping, selling, and delivery of the service to the customer. These units were created, however, for a single, more clearly defined task. Treasury was created to obtain funds, Corporate to sell loans, and Operations to process paper. The new strategy has created a flow of work that cuts across all units and asks them to reorient themselves. This is difficult. Ultimately, Amity was required to rethink its basic structure and move toward units that would be orga-nized around markets or sets of customers rather than around particular functions.

At Parkside, in a somewhat different situation, the medical cen-ter has become aware of a problem—the lack of well-coordinated, inte-grated, high-quality patient care. The task force has uncovered some interesting information, which will ultimately lead the medical center's senior management to realize that the center is not organized to deliver integrated patient care but to do research and teach effectively. However, the structure itself makes it impossible to identify a consistent set of phy-sicians, patients, staff, and support services with which it can work in order to focus on and coordinate improvement in the quality of care. The Parkside management finally recognized that large-scale and significant improvement in the quality of patient care would require a restructuring of the hospital into smaller units linked to departments of the medical school, with some support services decentralized into clusters of patient care units. Management also realized that a new job, that of unit man-ager, would have to be created in order to pull together the groups nec-essary for the delivery of high-quality care in each unit.

# DESIGN AS A LEVERAGE POINT

Both of these cases illustrate how organization design can be a key element influencing how organizations perform. Design is potentially a major leverage point that managers can use to shape patterns of performance. In fact, many senior managers consider themselves to be primarily architects of organizations. In a speech to marketing and sales managers, James Olsen, Vice-Chairman of AT&T, commented that:

> Your job is to be architects of systems, to design communications systems that meet customer needs. My job is, as an architect of organizations, to design organizations that will get the work done.

Why is organization design such a popular tool among managers? Why is the history of most organizations marked by series of reorganizations? Why have managers used organization design so extensively as a leverage point? Several reasons come to mind.

First, organization design is relatively easy to change. In many organizations, the structure is one of the few things that a manager can truly control. It is simple (deceptively so, as we shall see) to draw some boxes and lines on a piece of paper and announce a new structure. It is much more difficult to change behavior, modify culture, or develop new strategies.

It is not just the ease that motivates the use of design as a tool, however. The allure of design is that it can have great impact on an organization. For example, in the mid-1970s, when Citibank created a Consumer Services Group and pulled together under one person all of the different units providing banking services to individual customers, it assembled resources, talent, technology, and capital that resulted in a major thrust of the organization over the next ten years.

In addition, design can serve as a signal to direct attention to a particular set of issues or concerns. In the mid-1980s, when the Xerox Corporation decided to place a major, continuing emphasis on the quality of its products and services, one of its early steps was to create quality vice-presidents at the corporate and operating unit levels. The creation of these positions, the level at which they were designated, and the quality of the people put into the jobs called attention to the fact that something serious was being undertaken.

Similarly, managers can use design to put their personal stamp on an organization, particularly when a new manager comes into a position. In 1983, Walter Shipley became Chairman of Chemical Bank in New York. Shipley had a vision of the bank's senior management's working as a partnership, with a set of people sharing in the management of the whole institution. He signaled this very distinctly by announcing the appointment of not one, but three people, all with the title of President of Chemical Bank. The creation of three presidents was a design innovation that Shipley used to start putting his own stamp on the organization of Chemical Bank.

Similarly, design can be used to shape an organization's tone, or operating style. In 1984, Ted Brophy, Chairman of GTE, was anxious to create a sense of teamwork. A key step was the creation of a Corporate Policy Committee (there had previously been no senior group or committee), in which eight senior managers would meet once a week to discuss how they would work together. The committee as a structural device set a new tone for the organization, starting at the top.

Design can sometimes signal change. In 1982, AT&T charged William F. Buehler with building a new organization that would sell communications equipment and services to small and medium-sized businesses. In designing the organization, Buehler reduced the number of levels of hierarchy and drastically simplified the measurement and reporting systems, as a signal that the new organization would be less bureaucratic and more entrepreneurial in approaching its market.

Finally, managers are frequently forced to become involved in redesign by the process of mergers, acquisitions, or divestitures, which place them in the role of designers and redesigners, as pieces of organizations are either separated or put together. For example, literally thousands of managers have worked on organization design tasks as a consequence of the Bell System breakup.

## DESIGN AS A COMMON OCCURRENCE

Thus, design or redesign is a common occurrence in the life of an organization. Whether it is a new manager who takes over a small group and changes job assignments or a General Motors that undertakes a massive restructuring of its car divisions, structural changes are pervasive.

Despite the obvious impact of a new structure on an organization, managers' efforts to structure and design organizations are of vastly uneven quality. Some structural innovations stand out as significant advances in both the history of a particular company and in the development of organizational forms. Sloan's decentralized profit centers in General Motors, Ford's assembly line, and General Electric's strategic business units are examples of well-planned and well-implemented structural advances. For every success, however, there have been numerous situations in which restructuring or the development of a particular organization design was a prelude (along with other factors) to an organization's demise. There have also been situations in which constant reorganizations have led to confusion, diversion of energy, and decreased organizational effectiveness. For every design that displays a spark of genius or a truly new insight into social organization, there are ten misguided efforts that reflect no more thought than a couple of sketches on napkins over lunch.

With the possible exception of individual leadership, organization design may be the single most leveraged tool available to senior managers. Decisions about design determine where the organization will put its effort; influence the use of resources; define individual jobs; facilitate or constrain the accomplishment of work; motivate various types of job performance; and perhaps most importantly, shape the patterns of informal interactions and relationships that develop over time.

## WHY IS DESIGN SO UNEVEN?

Given the importance of an organization's design, why have so many design decisions been so poor? Part of the answer lies in looking, first, at the academic work on organization design and then at the practice of design as it frequently occurs in organizations.

For many years, design guidance from the academic world was composed primarily of the prescriptions of classical management theorists. These writers proposed "principles of management" that reflected neither the realities of current organizational life nor the findings of the empirical research on organizational behavior. Starting in the late 1960s and continuing through the 1970s, a growing body of literature focused on theoretically and empirically sound approaches to understanding organization structure.[1] While this research has provided valuable insights into the possible appropriate designs for different situations, it has, unfortunately, failed to address the pragmatic question of how managers might make design decisions germane to their particular situations. Thus, while progress has been made, there is still an absence of pragmatic tools to aid managers in making decisions about how to structure their organizations.

In the absence of useful guidance from the academic world, managers have relied on either their own common sense or the recommendations of management consultants who work with organizations on design projects. In practice, these approaches, while pragmatic, also tend to have a number of failings. First, they have tended to focus only on the technical aspects of design — the requirements to implement a strategy or to do the work — with scant consideration for individual needs and perceptions, informal organization issues, and patterns of organizational culture. As a result, many of these designs frequently are not implemented but remain as recommendations, sets of overhead transparencies in binders, permanently planted on bookshelves. A second type of problem with these pragmatic approaches is that they are often intuitive responses rather than thorough responses driven by systematic problem solving. Frequently, these intuitive responses are driven by personal or political factors with little regard for strategic or work requirements. One of the most frequent requirements specified for a design, for example, is "we have to create a job for everyone we currently have on the team." While these redesigns avoid conflict, they may do little to help the organization or individuals perform more effectively. Third, many of these pragmatic designs are solution-driven versus problem-driven. Frequently, a manager or consultant becomes familiar with a new organization design that is attractive, popular, or trendy (i.e., Matrix, SBUs, Lines of Business). The next step is to find a place to use the design. There is little concern with the problem supposedly being solved by the design. In these cases, a redesign is simply a symptom of managerial faddism.

## A BALANCED PERSPECTIVE

This book is an attempt to present a balanced approach to designing an organization. The book's underlying themes can be summarized as follows:

1. Organization design is part of the manager's job. Managers design and redesign organizations all the time. Therefore, most managers are organization designers.

2. Organization design involves a set of decisions about the shape, configuration, and features of the formal structure. Design is therefore a constant decision-making process that managers cycle through repeatedly.

3. Guidance in making more effective design decisions must balance the theoretical with the practical. Managers should benefit from the last twenty-five years of research and theory development on organization design, but the research-based tools must be put into a pragmatic form.

4. As managers make design decisions, they have to constantly balance two perspectives. One is the strategic, or task performance, perspective concerning how well the design will aid in implementing strategy and getting the work done. The second is

a social, or cultural, perspective, which focuses on the design's impact on the individual, interpersonal, and political aspects of organization life. Both perspectives must be considered in the design decision-making process.

The book focuses, then, on providing three things (see Figure 1-3). First, **concepts** for thinking about organizations and for thinking about organization design are presented. These concepts are to serve as a way of thinking systematically about the various issues in organization design. Second, some specific organization design **tools** are discussed. These tools will help in thinking about the different kinds of design decisions that are made by managers. Third, some specific **processes** for making design decisions are outlined.

## ORGANIZATION OF THE BOOK

The book begins by presenting concepts, moves to a discussion of some specific tools, and then shifts to a specific process for making design decisions. The remainder of the book considers special topics to address when selecting and implementing organization designs.

The most basic concepts are presented in Chapter 2. Organization

FIGURE 1-3    Focus of the Book

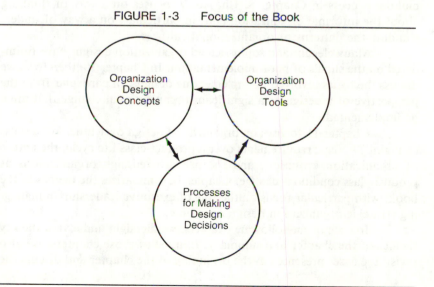

design decisions are not made in a vacuum. Designers need to consider all of the other "nondesign" elements of the organization. One way to keep all of these factors in mind is to have a general framework, or model, for thinking about organizations. One such model is presented in Chapter 2 and is used throughout the book as a means of focusing on the question of balance between strategic and human concerns in design.

Basic concepts of design are presented in Chapter 3, and a way of thinking about different types of design decisions (strategic and operational) is discussed. In Chapter 4, a specific model for organization design is presented. This model serves as the basic tool for applying the research on organization design to decision making. Chapters 5 and 6 elaborate on this model through a discussion of the two key decisions that managers must make about the basic shape of an organization: decisions about the formation of units, or groups, in the organization and decisions about how to coordinate, or link together, those groups. Chapter 7 discusses the question of centralization versus decentralization as an aspect of strategic organization design and focuses on managing line-staff relations.

The most specific guidance is provided in Chapter 8, in which a sequence, or process, for making decisions about design is outlined. This provides a means for managers to apply the concepts and tools in a systematic and orderly manner, which considers not only strategic issues but also works in the "softer" aspects of the organization.

Throughout the book there is an emphasis on the less formal and explicit aspects of organization. Having gone through the design decision-making process in Chapter 8, Chapter 9 focuses on a way of thinking about the informal organization and, in particular, on a way of understanding the patterns of organizational cultures.

Many elegant and sophisticated organization designs have floundered on the shoals of poor implementation. In Chapter 10, therefore, we discuss the issues involved in implementing designs, in particular from the perspective of a design as a significant organizational change that must be implemented.

Chapter 11 focuses on organization design over time. We discuss changing strategic requirements over a product-class life cycle, the nature of organization evolution, and the need to redesign organizations as product-class conditions change. Chapter 12 summarizes the themes of the book, with particular focus on the role of executive leadership in managing strategic organization design over time.

In each of the following chapters, we highlight and review the key themes of the chapter in a summary. In most of those chapters, we also revisit the cases presented at the beginning of the chapter and discuss the actions taken in light of the material presented in the body of the chapter. Our intent is to ground the concepts, models, and ideas in the reality of managers' facing real design decisions in actual organizations.

**Opening cases revisited:**

This first chapter began with two cases — Amity Bank and Parkside Hospital. While we will not "solve" these cases here, they do provide examples of situations in which at least part of the solution involves changes in organization design. In the case of Amity Bank, the new strategy puts many more demands on the organization for coordination across the boundaries of the different organizational units (Corporate Banking, Operations, and Treasury). At the minimum, Amity will need to design some kinds of mechanisms to link more effectively the activities of various people who are attempting to serve the needs of a particular customer but who reside in the different divisions of the Institutional Banking Group. If people just want to cooperate, that will probably not be enough. Specific devices to aid people in making linkages to others in different groups will probably have to be designed.

Similarly, Parkside Hospital is faced with the task of integrating the efforts of different people with different skills, different training, different disciplines, and different organizational locations. All of these people will have to coordinate their efforts if the goal of enhanced patient care is to be achieved. The problem is that each of the two halves of the medical center (the medical school and the hospital) is organized to meet its own individual goals, rather than to meet an over-arching common goal — quality patient care. The two halves of the organization do not fit together — they are not "plug compatible." A major rethinking of how each of the two halves organizes itself (including what are the major departments in each part of the organization), as well as an examination of how the different departments and groups fit together to deliver care, is required.

In this opening chapter, we have positioned organization design as a managerial problem, issue, and task. We have focused on how managers commonly make design decisions and the fact that, while design is not the answer to all problems in organizations, it frequently is an important component of significant efforts to enhance organizational effectiveness.

## NOTES

1. Examples of this work include: T. Burns and G. Stalker, *Management of Innovation*, (London: Tavistock, 1961); J. Galbraith, *Organization Design*, (Reading, MA: Addison-Wesley, 1977); R. Katz and D. Kahn, *Social Psychology of Organizations*, (New York: Wiley, 1966); P. Lawrence and J. Lorsch, *Organizations and Environments*, (Cambridge, MA: Harvard University Press, 1967); J. March and H. Simon, *Organizations*, (New York: Wiley, 1959); J. Pfeffer, *Organization Design*, (Arlington Heights, IL: AHM Publications, 1978); J. Thompson, *Organizations in Action*, (New York: McGraw-Hill, 1967); J. Woodward, *Industrial Organization*, (New York: Oxford University Press, 1962).

# 2

# A Conceptual Model
# for Thinking About
# Organizations

**Case:**

Landis & Co. is a large securities brokerage firm that has grown significantly over the past years through acquisition of other companies, both in the brokerage business and in related areas of the financial services industry. Although the senior management of Landis all grew up in the brokerage house, they became aware of the need to think about the business more broadly. In particular, they recognized the need to restructure their business in order to give the nonbrokerage parts of the organization the attention that they required, thus allowing the most senior levels to start Landis' evolution into a full-service financial services organization capable of competing with Sears, Merrill-Lynch, and other key players in the industry.

The chairman of Landis decided that the restructuring of the company was a key priority and devoted a good deal of time to the development of a new structure. For several months, he met once a week with his senior vice-presidents of strategic planning and human resources to work on the design of a new organization.

The day finally came when this small group felt that they had reached a good solution. The new design (see Figure 2-1) envisioned a holding company with key staff units in the corporate staff. Reporting to the holding company were four relatively autonomous business units—free-standing businesses. One of the particularly attractive features was that the new design involved taking a number of operations out of the brokerage house, which had been growing rapidly, thus keeping it at a more manageable size. In thinking about the competitive environment, the nature of the work that needed to be done, the strategies that were being developed, and the cost issues, this four-company solution made terrific sense. The group decided to start thinking about the next steps — how to announce and implement the new structure.

The next day, the chairman came into the office very troubled and called together his advisors. As they sat down, he got quickly to the point:

"I've been thinking about our new structure and I realize we have some big problems — two in particular. First, when I started to think about the team currently running the brokerage house would react to this idea, I realized that we have a very tough sell. They're going to see this as cutting away some important pieces of their turf. Frankly, I'm not sure that it's worth the fight. Second, I started to think about the four companies and whom we would put in place to run them. While we have a lot of bright and talented people here, most of them are really specialists. To be honest, I would be hard pressed to name four good general managers whom I would trust to run these companies."

## ORGANIZATION DESIGN — A QUESTION OF BALANCE

The Landis case is a clear illustration of how an organization designer must balance the strategic and task performance requirements of an organization against the realities of human behavior and interaction. While the designers in this case have developed a design that meets all of the requirements of the strategy and the organization's work, it clearly does not take into account some of the key political issues, as well as questions of individual capacity to make the design work.

What are the issues, or conflicting demands, that the organization designer must keep in mind? The designer should consider two sets of questions (see Figure 2-2). On one hand, the designer must consider how the structure will enable the organization to execute its various strategies and how the design will facilitate the management of the organization to ensure that the required work is accomplished. On the other hand, there is a second set of issues that, for now, we will broadly label as individual, social, or cultural. Here the focus is more on how the design will fit with or have an impact on the individuals who work for the organiza-

FIGURE 2-1    Landis & Co. — Proposed Organization

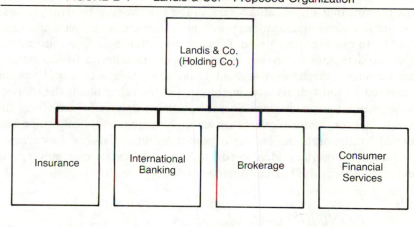

tion and the informal patterns of behavior (i.e., culture or politics) that have developed.

Both perspectives are valid, but each by itself is incomplete and will lead the designer into trouble. Those who consider only the strategic task performance issues are likely to design organizations that technically look effective but that somehow do not work, or are not implemented, or create as many new problems as they solve. On the other hand, those who consider only the individual/social/cultural perspective may create organizations in which many people feel satisfied but which are never able to come to grips with key strategic issues nor deal effectively with the work or work flows.

To some extent, these diverse perspectives reflect very different

FIGURE 2-2    Two Design Perspectives

| Strategy/Task Performance | Individual/Social/Cultural |
|---|---|
| — Design supports the implementation of strategy. | — How will existing people fit into the design? |
| — Design facilitates the flow of work. | — How will the design affect power relations among different groups? |
| — Design permits effective managerial control. | — How will the design fit with people's values and beliefs? |
| — Design creates doable, measurable jobs. | — How will the design affect the tone and operating style of the organization? |

underlying views about the fundamental nature of organizations, or about the reasons that organizations exist in the first place. The strategic/task perspective views organizations purely as devices created to get work done, that is, to execute strategies and create value, thus benefiting customers, shareholders, and the society at large. An organization is fundamentally an economic mechanism created to achieve ends that could not be achieved by individuals working alone. On the other hand, the individual/cultural perspective views organizations as devices for satisfying the needs, desires, and aspirations of various stakeholders, both inside and outside of the organization. An organization thus exists for the purposes of meeting those individual needs, aiding in the exercise of power, and expressing individual or collective values.

## CONCEPTUAL MODELS
## AS MANAGERIAL TOOLS

Obviously, both perspectives are valid. An organization is a technical and economic entity, but it is also a social process created by those people of whom it is comprised. It is neither a fully rational actor nor a fluid, anarchic, nonpurposive organism. It is a combination, or balance, of both.

What does all this mean for the organization designer? It implies that the designer must have a way of thinking about this balance. The designer must be able to keep in mind the various aspects of organizational life. The designer needs a tool to help him or her think about organizations as a whole, while structuring the formal, or explicit, parts of those organizations. One tool is the conceptual framework, or model. A model is a theory that indicates which factors (in an organization, for example) are most important. It also shows how these factors are related—that is, which factors or combination of factors causes other factors to change. In a sense, then, a model is a roadmap that can be used to make sense of the terrain of organizational behavior.

The models we use are critical because they guide our analysis and action. In any organizational situation, problem solving (including solving the problem of organization design) involves the collection of information about the problem, the interpretation of that information to determine specific problem types and causes, and the development of appropriate action plans. The models that individuals use influence the kind of data they collect and the kind they ignore; models guide people's approach to analyzing or interpreting the data they have; finally, models help people choose their course of action.

Indeed, anyone who has been exposed to an organization already has some sort of implicit model. People develop these roadmaps over time, building on their own experiences. For example, in Chapter 1, we mentioned the example of Walter Shipley, Chairman of Chemical Bank in New York, who wanted to create a management team that was like a partnership. Where did this idea come from? Shipley has stated numerous times that he was impressed with the partnership concept, which he saw operate and he experienced through his father, who was a partner at Brown Brothers Harriman, a well-known investment banking partnership. Through his experiences, Shipley had developed a model for thinking about how organizations might be structured.

Shipley's model was explicit. He was aware of it, talked about it, and could describe it. Most of the time, people's models of organization are implicit, or unstated, but they still guide behavior. They do, however, vary in quality, validity, and sophistication, depending on the nature and extent of the experiences of the model builder, as well as his or her perceptiveness and ability to conceptualize and generalize from experiences.

We are not solely dependent, however, on the implicit and experience-based models that individuals develop. Since there has been extensive research and theory development on the subject of organizational behavior over the last four decades, it is possible to use scientifically developed explicit models for analyzing behavior and solving organizational problems.

In this chapter, a general model of organizations will be described as a basic tool for understanding the dynamics of the organization, and its implications for making organization design decisions will be discussed. This general model attempts to provide a framework for thinking about the organization as a total system. It provides a context for looking more specifically at design. (A more specific organization design model will be described in Chapter 4.) The model's major premise is that for organizations to be effective, their subparts, or components, must be consistently structured and managed—they must approach a state of congruence.

In the next section of this chapter, we will discuss the basic view of organizations that underlies the model—systems theory. In the following section, we will present and discuss the model itself. Subsequently, a general approach to using the model for organizational problem analysis will be outlined. Finally, we will draw some basic conclusions about the design of organizations based on this general model.

## A BASIC VIEW OF ORGANIZATIONS

There are many different ways of thinking about organizations. When a manager is asked to "draw a picture of an organization," he or she typically draws a version of a pyramidal organization chart. This model views the stable, formal relationships among the jobs and work units as the most critical factors of an organization. Although this is one way to think about organizations, it is a very limited view that excludes such factors as leadership behavior, the impact of the environment, informal relations, and power distribution. Such a model can capture only a fraction of what actually goes on in organizations. Its perspective is narrow and static.

The past two decades have seen a growing consensus that a viable alternative to the classic static models of organizations is to envision the organization as a social system. This approach stems from the observation that social phenomena display many of the same characteristics as natural or mechanical systems. In particular, a number of theorists have argued that organizations can be better understood if they are considered as dynamic and "open" social systems.[1]

What is a system? Most simply stated, a system is a set of interrelated elements—that is, a change in one element affects other elements. An **open system** interacts with its environment; it is more than just a set of interrelated elements. Rather, these elements make up a mechanism that takes input from the environment, transforms the input, and produces output. At the most general level, it should be easy to visualize organizations as systems. For example, a manufacturing plant is made up of different but related components (departments, jobs, and technologies). The plant receives input from the environment—labor, raw material, production orders—and transforms these inputs into products.

Organizations display a number of basic systems characteristics. Some of the most critical are:

> **Internal interdependence**—Changes in one component of an organization frequently have repercussions for other parts; the pieces are interconnected. Again, as in the manufacturing plant cited, changes made in one element (for example, the skill levels of employees) will affect other elements (the productiveness of equipment, the speed or quality of production activities, or the nature of supervision needed).
>
> **Capacity for feedback**—that is, information about the output that can be used to control the system. Organizations can correct errors and even change themselves because of this characteristic. If, in our plant example, management receives information that product quality is declining, it can use this information to identify factors in the system itself that contribute to the problem. However, unlike mechanized systems, feedback information does

not always lead to correction. Organizations have the potential to use feedback for self-correction, but they do not always realize this potential.

**Equilibrium** — that is, a state of balance. When an event puts the system out of balance, it reacts by moving to bring itself back into balance. If one work group in our plant example were suddenly to increase its performance dramatically, it would throw the system out of balance. This group would be making increasing demands on the groups that supply it with the information or materials it needs; groups that work with the high-performing group's output would feel the pressure of work-in-process inventory's piling up. If a type of incentive is in effect, other groups might perceive inequity as this one group begins to earn more. We can predict that some actions would be taken to put the system back into balance. Either the rest of the plant would be changed to increase production and thus be put back in balance with the single group, or (more likely) there would be pressure on this group to modify its behavior in line with the performance levels of the rest of the system (by removing workers or limiting supplies, for example). Somehow the system would develop the energy to move back toward a state of equilibrium.

**Equifinality** — different system configurations can lead to the same end, or to the same type of input/output conversion. There is no universal, or "one best," way to organize. This point is particularly critical to keep in mind when designing organizations. While there is usually not one best way to structure an organization, there clearly are some ways that are better than others. The challenge is to identify that set of designs that is relatively comparable based on technical concerns and then make the ultimate choice based on other factors (individual, political, or cultural).

**Adaptation** — For a system to survive, it must maintain a favorable balance of input and output transactions with the environment, or it will run down. If our plant produces a product for which there are fewer applications over time, the company that owns the plant must adapt to new demands and develop new products; otherwise, the plant will ultimately have to close its doors. Any system, therefore, must adapt as environmental conditions change. Prosperous organizations can fail if they do not respond to environmental changes.

Thus, open systems theory provides a way of thinking about the organization in more complex and dynamic terms. Although the theory provides a valuable basic perspective, it is limited as a problem-solving tool because it is too abstract for use in day-to-day analysis of organizational behavior problems. Owing to the level of abstraction in systems theory, we need to develop a more specific and pragmatic model based on the concepts of the open systems paradigm.

## A CONGRUENCE MODEL OF ORGANIZATIONAL BEHAVIOR

Given the level of abstraction of open systems theory, our job is to develop a model that reflects the basic systems concepts and characteristics but that is more specific and thus more viable as an analytic tool. We will describe a model that specifies the critical inputs, the major outputs, and the transformation processes that characterize organizational functioning.

This model puts its greatest emphasis on the transformation process and specifically illustrates the critical characteristic of system interdependence. It views organizations as constructed of components that interact. These components exist in states of relative balance and consistency—they "fit" with each other. The parts of an organization can fit together well and function effectively, or they can fit poorly and lead to problems, dysfunctions, and performance below potential. This **congruence model of organizational behavior** is based on the degree to which components fit together—the congruence among the components. The effectiveness of an organization is a reflection of the quality of the congruence of the key components.[2]

It is important to remember that we are concerned about creating a model for behavioral systems of an organization—the system of elements that ultimately produces behavior patterns and, in turn, organizational performance. Put simply, we must understand the input with which the system has to work, the output it must produce, the major components of the transformation process, and the ways in which these components interact.

### Context

Context includes the elements that, at any one point in time, make up the "givens" facing the organization—the material with which the organization has to work. There are several types of contextual factors, each of which presents a set of givens to the organization (see Figure 2-3 for an overview of organization context).

FIGURE 2-3   Organizational Context

| Input | Environment | Resources | History | Strategy |
|---|---|---|---|---|
| Definition | All factors, including institutions, groups, individuals, events, and so on, that are outside the organization being analyzed but that have a potential impact on that organization | Various assets to which the organization has access, including human resources, technology, capital, information, and so on, as well as less tangible resources (recognition in the market, and so forth) | The patterns of past behavior, activity, and effectiveness of the organization that may affect current organizational functioning | The stream of decisions about how organizational resources will be configured to meet the demands, constraints, and opportunities within the context of the organization's history |
| Critical Features for Analysis | 1. What demands does the environment make on the organization? <br> 2. How does the environment put constraints on organizational action? | 1. What is the relative quality of the different resources to which the organization has access? <br> 2. To what extent are resources fixed rather than flexible in their configuration(s)? | 1. What have been the major stages or phases of the organization's development? <br> 2. What is the current impact of such historical factors as strategic decisions, acts of key leaders, crises, and core values and norms? | 1. How has the organization defined its core mission, including the markets it serves and the products/services it provides to these markets? <br> 2. On what basis does it compete? <br> 3. What supporting strategies has the organization employed to achieve the core mission? <br> 4. What specific objectives have been set for organizational output? |

Strategy → Objectives/Tactics

The first contextual factor is the **environment**, or factors outside of the organization. Every organization exists within a larger environment, which includes individuals, groups, other organizations, and larger technological and social forces — all of which have a potentially powerful impact on how the organization performs. Specifically, the environment includes markets (clients or customers), suppliers, governmental and regulatory bodies, technological conditions, labor unions, competitors, financial institutions, and special interest groups. Three critical features of the environment affect organizational functioning. First, the environment makes demands on the organization. For example, it may require certain products or services at certain levels of quality or quantity. Market pressures are particularly important here. Second, the environment may place constraints on organizational action. It may limit the activities in which an organization may engage. These constraints range from the limitations imposed by scarce capital or technology to prohibitions set by government regulations. Third, the environment provides opportunities for the organization to explore. When we analyze an organization, we must consider these factors in its environment and determine how they, singly or collectively, create demands, constraints, or opportunities.

The second contextual factor is the organization's **resources**. Any organization has a range of assets to which it has access. These include employees, technology, capital, and information. Resources may also include less tangible assets, such as the perception of the organization in the marketplace or a positive organizational climate. Organizations can shape or deploy resources in various ways. For the purpose of analysis, two features are of primary interest: the relative quality of those resources, or their value in the context of the current or future environment, and the extent to which resources can be reshaped, or their flexibility.

The third contextual factor is the organization's **history**. There is growing evidence that the way an organization functions today is greatly influenced by past events. It is particularly important to understand the major stages, or phases, of an organization's development over time, as well as the current impact of past events — for example, prior strategic decisions, the behavior of key leaders, the nature of past crises and the organization's responses to them, and the evolution of core values and norms.

Environmental conditions, organizational resources, and history are contextual factors that cannot be changed in the short run — they are givens that provide the setting within which managers make strategic decisions. **Organization strategy** is reflected in those consequential decisions that allocate scarce resources against demands, constraints, and opportunities of a given environment (review Figure 2-3).

More explicitly, strategy can be defined as specific choices of products, markets, technology, and distinctive competence. Given explicit attention to environmental opportunities and threats, organizational strengths and weaknesses, and organization history, managers need to make such decisions as what products do we offer, to what markets, and how we will distinguish our firm (e.g., first-mover, low-cost producer, or niche-player). These long-term strategic objectives must then be factored into a set of internally consistent shorter-term **objectives** and **supporting strategies**, or tactics.

Decisions on products, markets, technology, and distinctive competence are the most important decisions for managers. Those organizations that make inappropriate strategic decisions will underperform or fail. No amount of organization design can help an ill-conceived strategy. However, given a viable strategy and internally consistent objectives, management's challenge is to build an organization to accomplish those strategic objectives. Strategy, then, determines both the nature of the work and critical organization outputs.

## Output

Output is what the organization produces, how it performs, and how effective it is. There has been much discussion about the definition of an effective organization. For our purposes, however, it is possible to identify several critical aspects of organizational output. Firstly, we need to think about system output at different levels. In addition to the system's basic output (that is, the product and services or economic return), we need to think about other types of output that contribute to organizational performance, such as the functioning of groups or units within the organization or the functioning of individual organization members.

At the organizational level, three factors must be kept in mind when evaluating organizational performances: (1) goal attainment, or how well the organization meets its objectives (usually as specified by strategy), (2) resource utilization, or how well the organization makes use of available resources (not just whether it meets its goals, but whether it realizes all of its potential performance and whether it achieves its goals by building resources or by "burning them up"), and (3) adaptability, or whether the organization continues to position itself in a favorable position vis-a-vis its environment—that is, whether it is capable of adapting to environmental changes.

Obviously, the functioning of organizational units (i.e., departments or divisions) contributes to the organizational-level output. Organizational output is also influenced by individual behavior, and certain individual-level output (affective reactions such as satisfaction, stress, or experienced quality of working life) may be desired output in and of itself.

## The organization as a transformation process

So far, we've defined the nature of the input and output of the organizational system. This leads us to the transformation process. Given an environment, a set of resources, and history, the question is how to implement a strategy to produce effective performance at the individual, group, and organizational levels.

In this model, the organization and its major components are the fundamental means for transforming energy and information from input into output. To understand this process, we need to identify the key components of the organization and the underlying critical dynamic.

## Organizational components

There are many different ways of thinking about what makes up an organization. The challenge is to find useful approaches for describing organizations, for simplifying complex phenomena, and for identifying patterns in what may at first seem to be random activity. This model views four major components of organizations: (1) the task, (2) the individuals, (3) the formal organizational arrangements, and (4) the informal organization (see Figure 2-4 for overviews of these components).

The first component is the organization's **task**—the basic and inherent work to be done by the organization and its units, or the activity in which the organization is engaged, particularly in light of its strategy. The emphasis is on the specific work activities, or functions, that need to be done and their inherent characteristics (as opposed to the work characteristics resulting from how the work is organized, or structured, in this particular organization at this particular time). Task analysis would include a description of the basic work and work flows. This analysis must capture the different kinds of required tasks and the specific work flows, as well as assess their characteristics—for example, the knowledge or skills demanded by the work, the kinds of rewards it provides, its degree of uncertainty, and its inherent constraints (such as critical time demands and cost constraints). Since it is assumed that a primary (although clearly not the only) reason for the organization's existence is to perform the task consistent with strategy, the task is the starting point for analysis. As we will see, the assessment of the adequacy of other components depends to a large degree on an understanding of the nature of the tasks to be per-

FIGURE 2-4   The Four Organizational Components

| Component | Task | Individual | Formal Organizational Arrangements | Informal Organization |
|---|---|---|---|---|
| Definition | The basic and inherent work to be done by the organization and its parts | The characteristics of individuals in the organization | The various structures, processes, methods that are formally created to get individuals to perform tasks | The emerging arrangements including structures, processes, relationships |
| Critical Features of Each Component | — Degree of uncertainty associated with the work, including such factors as interdependence and routineness<br>— Types of skill and knowledge demands the work poses<br>— Types of rewards the work inherently can provide<br>— Constraints on performance demands inherent in the work (given a strategy) | — Knowledge and skills individuals have<br>— Individual needs and preferences<br>— Perceptions and expectancies<br>— Background factors<br>— Demography | — Grouping of functions, structure of units<br>— Coordination and control mechanisms<br>— Job design<br>— Work environment<br>— Human resource management systems<br>— Reward systems<br>— Physical location | — Leader behavior<br>— Norms, values<br>— Intragroup relations<br>— Intergroup relations<br>— Informal working arrangements<br>— Communication and influence patterns<br>— Key roles<br>— Climate<br>— Power, politics |

formed. This is particularly critical in analyzing the organization for design or redesign. Since we organize to get work done, it is critical to understand the nature and significant characteristics of that work and work flows.

A second component of organizations involves the **individuals** who perform tasks. The issue here is identifying the nature and characteristics of the employees or members. The most critical aspects to consider include the nature of individual knowledge and skills; the different needs or preferences of individuals; the perceptions or expectancies that they develop; and other demographic factors, such as age or sex, that potentially influence individual behavior.

The third component is the **formal organizational arrangements**. These include the structures, processes, methods, and procedures that are explicitly and formally developed to get individuals to perform tasks consistent with organizational strategy. The broad term *organizational arrangements* encompasses a number of factors, which we will explore in more depth in the next chapter. Our focus here, however, is on the formal arrangements that are explicitly designed and specified.

The final component is the **informal organization**. Despite the set of formal organizational arrangements that exists in any organization, another set of arrangements tends to emerge over time. These arrangements are usually implicit and unwritten, but they can exert considerable influence on behavior. Such arrangements are frequently referred to as the *informal organization* (and more recently have been described by the term *organizational culture*). They include the structures, processes, and arrangements that emerge while the organization is operating. These arrangements sometimes complement formal organizational arrangements by providing structures to aid work accomplishment. In other situations, they may emerge in reaction to the formal structure—to protect individuals from it. Thus, they may either aid or hinder organizational performance.

A number of aspects of the informal organization have a critical effect on behavior. The behavior of leaders (as opposed to the formal creation of leader jobs/roles/positions) is an important feature of the informal organization, as are common values and beliefs and the relationships that develop within and between groups. In addition, various types of informal working arrangements (including rules, procedures, and methods) develop. Finally, various communication, influence, and political patterns combine to create an informal organization.

An organization can therefore be thought of as a set of components—the task, the individuals, the organizational arrangements, and the informal organization. In any system, however, the critical question is not what are the components, but what is the nature of their interaction and how does the relationship among the components affect how they combine to produce output.

## The concept of congruence

A relative degree of congruence and consistency exists between each pair of organizational components. The congruence between two components is defined as *the degree to which the needs, demands, goals, objectives, and/or structures of one component are consistent with the needs, demands, goals, objectives, and/or structures of another component.*

Congruence, therefore, is a measure of how well pairs of components fit together. Consider, for example, two components: the task and the individual. At the simplest level, the task presents skill and knowledge demands on individuals who would perform it. At the same time, the individuals available to do the tasks have certain characteristics (their levels of skill and knowledge). Obviously, if an individual's characteristics match the demands of the task, the performance will be more effective. Obviously, too, the individual-task congruence relationship encompasses more factors than just knowledge and skill. Similarly, each congruence relationship in the model has its own specific characteristics. Research and theory can guide the assessment of fit in each relationship. For an overview of the critical elements of each congruence relationship, see Figure 2-5.

## The congruence hypothesis

The aggregate model, or whole organization, displays a relatively high or low degree of system congruence in the same way that each pair of components has a high or low degree of congruence. The basic hypothesis of the model is as follows: Other things being equal, the greater the total degree of congruence or fit among the various components, the more effective will be the organization—effectiveness being defined as the degree to which actual organizational output is similar to expected or planned output, as specified by strategy.

The basic dynamic of congruence sees the organization as most effective when its pieces fit together. If we also consider strategy, this view expands to include the fit between the organization and its larger environment; an organization is most effective when its strategy is consistent with its environment (in light of organizational resources and history) and when the organizational components are congruent with the task necessary to implement that strategy.

FIGURE 2-5     Definitions of Fit Among Components

| Fit | Issues |
| --- | --- |
| Individual/Organization | How are individual needs met by the organizational arrangements?<br>Do individuals hold clear perceptions of organizational structures? Is there a convergence of individual and organizational goals? |
| Individual/Task | How are individual needs met by the tasks? Do individuals have skills and abilities to meet task demands? |
| Individual/Informal Organization | How are individual needs met by the informal organization? How does the informal organization make use of individual resources consistent with informal goals? |
| Task/Organization | Are organizational arrangements adequate to meet the demands of the task? Do organizational arrangements motivate behavior that is consistent with task demands? |
| Task/Informal Organization | Does the informal organization structure facilitate task performance? Does it help meet the demands of the task? |
| Organization/Informal Organization | Are the goals, rewards, and structures of the informal organization consistent with those of the formal organization? |

One important implication of the congruence hypothesis is that organization problem analysis (or diagnosis) involves description of the system, identification of problems, and analysis of fit to determine the causes of problems. The model also implies that various configurations of the key components can be used to obtain output (consistent with the systems characteristic of equifinality). Therefore, the question is not how to find the "one best way of managing," but how to find effective combinations of components that will lead to congruence among them. The process of identifying and diagnosing fit is not necessarily intuitive. A number of conditions that lead to congruence have been defined in the research literature. Thus, in many cases, fit can be defined and even quantified.

The congruence model provides a general organizing framework; however organization designers will need other, more specific models to define high and low congruence. In particular, the organization designer will need a more specific model to define the relationship among the formal organizational arrangements and the other components (that more specific model will be presented in Chapter 4).

In summary, then, we have described a general model for the analysis of organizations (see Figure 2-6). The organization is seen as a system and, in particular, as a process that transforms input into output, a process driven by relations among the four basic components. The critical dynamic is the fit, or congruence, among the components. We now turn our attention to the question of how to use this model for analyzing organizational problems. In subsequent chapters, we will use the model as a way of thinking about the context of design decisions.

## A PROCESS FOR ORGANIZATIONAL PROBLEM ANALYSIS

The conditions that face organizations frequently change; consequently, managers are required to continually engage in problem identification and problem-solving activities. Therefore, managers need to gather data on organizational performance, compare the data with desired performance levels, identify the causes of problems, choose and develop action plans, and, finally, implement and evaluate these action plans. Such phases can be viewed as parts of a generic problem-solving process. For long-term organizational viability, some type of problem-solving process must operate continuously.

Experience in using the congruence model for problem solving in actual organizational setting has led to the development of an approach to using the model based on these generic problem-solving processes (see Figure 2-7). In this section, we will "walk through" this process, describing each step and discussing how the model can be used at each stage:

1. **Identify symptoms:** In any situation, initial information (symptomatic data) may indicate that there are problems, but not what the problems, or their causes, are. Symptomatic data are important because the symptoms may indicate where to look for more complete data.

2. **Specify input:** Once the symptoms are identified, the starting point for analysis is to identify the system and the environment in which it functions. This means collecting data about the nature of the environment, about the organization's type of resources, and about the critical aspects of the organization's his-

FIGURE 2-6    A Congruence Model for Diagnosing Organizational Behavior

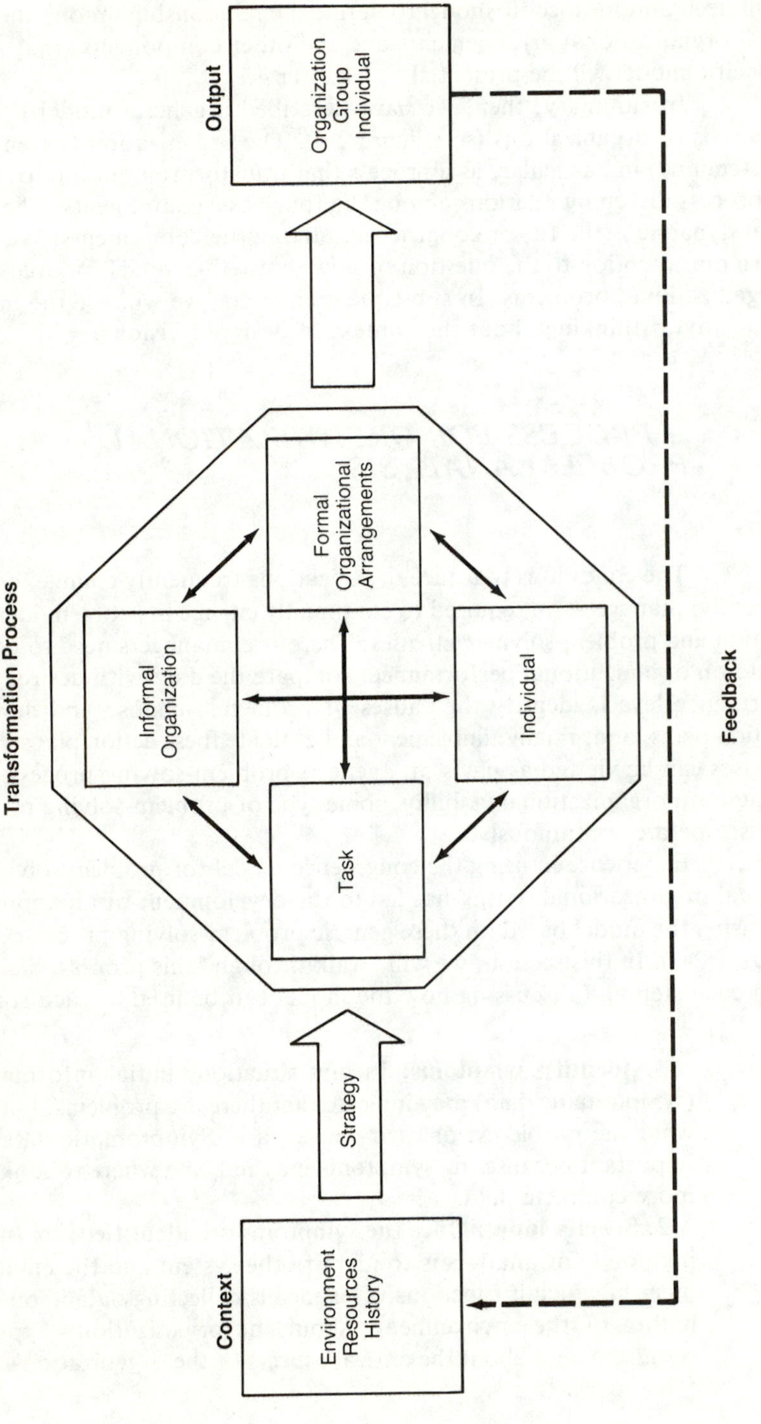

**Output**

Organization
Group
Individual

**Transformation Process**

Formal
Organizational
Arrangements

Informal
Organization

Individual

Task

**Strategy**

**Context**

Environment
Resources
History

**Feedback**

FIGURE 2-7      Steps in Organizational Problem Analysis

| Step | Explanation |
| --- | --- |
| 1. Identify symptoms | List data indicating possible existence of problems. |
| 2. Specify input | Identify the system.<br>Determine nature of environment, resources, and history.<br>Identify critical aspects of strategy. |
| 3. Identify output | Identify data that defines the nature of output at various levels (individual, group/unit, organization) — should include desired output (from strategy) and actual output being obtained. |
| 4. Identify problems | Identify areas where there are significant and meaningful differences between desired and actual output. To the extent possible, identify penalties, i.e., specific costs (actual and opportunity costs) associated with each problem. |
| 5. Describe components of the organization | Describe basic nature of each of the four components with emphasis on its critical features. |
| 6. Assess congruence (fit) | Analyze relative congruence among components (draw on more specific models as needed). |
| 7. Generate hypotheses | Analyze to associate fit with specific problems. |
| 8. Identify action steps | Indicate what possible actions might deal with causes of problems. |

tory. Input analysis also involves identifying the organization's overall strategy—its core mission, supporting strategies, and objectives.

3. **Identify output:** The third step is to analyze the organization's output at the individual, group, and organizational levels. Output analysis involves two elements: (1) defining the desired or planned output through strategic analysis that explicitly or implicitly defines what the organization wants to achieve in terms of output and (2) collecting data that indicate the type of output the organization is actually achieving.

4. **Identify problems:** Problems are defined as significant differences between planned output and actual output. Such problems might be discrepancies in organizational performance, group functioning, or individual behavior and affective reactions. These

data tell us what problems exist but do not indicate the causes. (Note: where data are available, it is frequently useful to identify the costs associated with the problems or the penalties incurred by not fixing the problems. Penalties might be actual costs, such as increased expenses, or opportunity costs, such as revenue lost because of the problem.)

5. **Describe organizational components:** At this step, the analysis to determine the causes of problems begins. Data are collected about the nature of each of the four major organizational components, including information about the component and its critical features. However, not all problems have organizational, or internal, causes. Problems may be the result of such strategic causes as a shift in environment, a new competitor, or a poor strategy. It is important to test for strategic causes before focusing too intently on organizational causes. Otherwise, the organization is in danger of becoming more effective at doing the wrong thing.

6. **Assess congruence (fit):** Using the data collected in step 5 as well as applicable specific models or theories, an assessment is made of the nature of the congruence among the various components.

7. **Generate hypotheses about problem causes:** Once the components are described and their congruence assessed, the next step is to link the congruence analysis with the problem identification done in step 4. After analyzing to determine which are the poorer fits that seem to be associated with or account for the identified output problems, one can describe the factors or combinations of factors that contribute to each problem. Then one can use available data to test whether these are indeed the key factors responsible for the problems, and thus leverage points for bringing about improvement.

8. **Identify action steps:** The final step in problem analysis is to identify possible action steps. These steps might range from specific changes to deal with relatively obvious problems to more extensive data collection designed to test hypotheses about relatively more complex problems.

In addition, some further steps must be considered. After possible actions are identified, problem solving involves predicting the consequence of various actions, choosing a course of action, implementing it, and evaluating its impact. It is, of course, important to have a general diagnostic framework to monitor the effects of various courses of action.

# SUMMARY — IMPLICATIONS OF THE MODEL FOR DESIGN

**Opening case revisited:**

We began this chapter by discussing the dilemma that faced the chairman of Landis & Co., a brokerage firm. As you remember, a recommendation had been developed that involved the creation of four free-standing businesses. The chairman was concerned because of the potential reactions of the team currently running the brokerage house, as well as the more pressing problem of a lack of qualified general managers to run the four businesses.

Faced with this dilemma, the group spent two hours discussing these and other issues and finally reached an agreement. The structure would be implemented in stages. The first stage would involve the creation of two major companies, each to be headed by one of the available high quality general managers. One of the two companies would preserve most of what the brokerage house currently had. Over time, the evolution from two to four companies would be managed as people became more comfortable with new ways of thinking about the business and as new general managers obtained more experience. As we have pointed out in this chapter, the solution recognized that the organization is composed of both formal and informal elements, combined with work to be done and people to do that work. An effective and workable design solution had to balance the requirements of those different sides of organizational life.

This general model of organizations provides an analytic context for making design decisions. In the language of the congruence model, the job of the general manager is to develop and implement strategies. The first step is to develop, test, and formulate strategies that the organization could implement, given its history, resources, environment, and internal capacities (including individual needs and culture). The second step in the manager's job is to implement strategies through the creation, building, shaping, maintaining, and sustaining of an organization. This means constantly defining the key tasks to be performed, making sure that individuals are capable of and are motivated toward performing those tasks, and developing formal and informal organizational arrangements that are congruent with strategy and work requirements; fit well with the nature of the individuals; and are consistent.

Fundamentally, organization design involves configuring the formal organization to support the implementation of strategy. However, at the same time and of equal import, organization design involves fitting the formal organization with individuals and informal organization. One can think of this as two axes of the model (see Figure 2-6) which correspond to the two perspectives that require balancing. As we continue to develop concepts and tools, we will refer to this model and the concepts of balance and trade-offs. We are now ready to look at what we mean by *design* and what is broadly involved in making design decisions.

## *NOTES*

1. D. Katz and R. Kahn, *Social Psychology of Organizations*, (New York: Wiley, 1966); K. Weick, *Social Psychology of Organizing*, (Reading, MA: Addison-Wesley, 1969); J. March and H. Simon, *Organizations*, (New York: Wiley, 1959).

2. Other similar approaches include: J. Galbraith, *Organization Design*, (Reading, MA: Addison-Wesley, 1977); T. Peters and R. Waterman. *In Search of Excellence*, (New York: Harper & Row, 1982); H. Leavitt, "Applied Organizational Change in Industry," in J. March, *Handbook of Organizations*, (Chicago: Rand McNally, 1965); N. Tichy, *Managing Strategic Change*, (New York: Wiley, 1983).

# 3

# Basic Concepts
# of Organization Design

**Case:**

The planning director of a major product division of a large chemical company had just spent a half hour listening to her boss, the division general manager, outline a proposal for reorganizing the division. The planning director looked down at the conference table. There sat the proposed design in front of her. It was obviously something that had been produced by a copying machine, but it was only after several minutes that she figured out the strange markings and patterns—she was looking at an organization chart that had been constructed on a paper dinner napkin. The folds, creases, holes, and incidental food stains embellished the chart's rough boxes and lines.

More seriously, the planning director was stumped. She could not figure out the rationale for the new organization. Each time she thought she had figured out what her boss was trying to do with the new structure, she would see something that did not quite fit. Finally she pushed herself to ask, "What exactly are you trying to accomplish with this reorganization?" The division general manager looked at the planner for a moment and then said, "Oh, I was just thinking about how we might shake things up a little. If you really want to know, I was open to anything as long as it didn't create problems. I have twelve people reporting directly to me now, so I thought of different ways that I could organize with twelve jobs reporting to the general manager."

## INTRODUCTION

It is not surprising that many organization designs first emerge as diagrams written on napkins, scraps of paper, or backs of envelopes. Many managers like to play around with design. As we mentioned earlier, it is one of the easier things to change and is clearly within the mandate of most managerial jobs. It is also frequently an intuitive, creative process. However, the intuitive, creative aspects may dominate to the extent that the manager does not systematically analyze the factors that should influence a design decision or does not consider its potential consequences. The decision-making process shapes the content of the decision, so organizations can be shaped by the size and configuration of a napkin or constrained by such decision rules as "if I have twelve reports now, I have to design an organization with twelve reports." Managers often feel that the design work is done when the napkin-based drawing is turned into a graphically impressive organization chart. They forget that there is more to a design than a set of boxes and lines on a piece of paper.

All this would be humorous if it did not have such a large potential impact. The scrawlings of senior managers often bring about major consequences for the organization, commencing the movement of people, assets, jobs, and units. When the underlying process to find an effective design is one of trial and error, each new napkin drawing can have a considerable cost.

In this chapter, we will build on the organizational model presented in Chapter 2 and use it to provide some basic definitions of design and some insights into the types of design decisions that managers make. We will first focus on the role and function of design within the context of the general organizational model. Next, we will define the elements of design. Third, we will attempt to answer the question of when to significantly redesign an organization. Finally, we will present a way of thinking about the different types of design decisions.

## ORGANIZATION DESIGN IN THE CONTEXT OF THE GENERAL MODEL

If we think about organizations in the terms of the congruence model, what must a manager who wants to implement a strategy think about? (Let us assume for a moment that the manager has done the appropriate analysis so that the strategy is adequate.) First, the manager should consider how the organization's work must change. How will the tasks change or how will the constraints on the task be modified? Second, the manager should think about the individuals in the organization and whether they have the skills, interest, and capacity to perform the work consistent with the strategy. Third, the manager might examine the informal organization, or culture, and see what types of values, beliefs, norms, leadership patterns, and arrangements exist and whether they will aid or hinder the performance of the work. Finally, the manager might consider the formal organizational arrangements — the various explicit structures and processes that have been created to get the individuals to perform tasks.

In practice, once the work requirements are defined, managers tend to gravitate toward the formal organizational arrangements as a tool, rather than toward other components. Why? First, the organizational arrangements are easier to manipulate directly than are the informal organization, or individual, components. Except in new organizations, a manager usually inherits a set of members. There are limits to how much their attitudes, values, skills, and capacities can be changed, and change takes time. Similarly, there are limits on the extent to which people can be replaced or moved. Finding the right new people is often difficult, and there are major implications concerning the psychological contract, or agreements, that people have about work and job security. Even in the best, least constrained situation, significant change in the composition of the individuals in an organization takes time.

The informal organization is equally difficult to impact directly. An informal organization develops over time and has a certain degree of resistance to change. As we will discuss later (in Chapters 8 and 9), implementing changes in an organization's culture is much easier to talk about than to do. Again, even effective informal organization changes in large organizations can take years.

The second reason that managers gravitate toward formal organizational arrangements is that they can have impact on patterns of behavior, activity, and performance. Indeed, the formal organizational arrangements can directly and indirectly affect the other components. For example, formal job definitions, hiring processes, and training programs can significantly influence the capacities of the individuals to do the tasks over time. The formal organizational structure, the composition of key committees, and the design of the measurement and rewards system can greatly influence the informal arrangements and patterns that develop.

The organizational arrangements also have some very powerful direct impact on how people perform work and act within the organization. First, the organizational arrangements can **motivate behavior**. Through the definition of jobs, the creation of goals, the development of measures, and the use of reward systems, people can be directed and energized to behave in certain ways. Second, the organizational arrangements can **facilitate behavior**. Once someone is motivated to behave in a certain way, the arrangements can help him or her do so. By providing methods and procedures, by placing the person in proximity to others with whom the person needs to communicate, and by providing necessary information, the formal organization can be facilitative—that is, it can help people perform tasks. Third, the organizational arrangements can **constrain behavior**. By limiting information, by building in formal procedures, and by separating certain groups or units from each other, the formal organization can limit what people can do and prevent them from spending time and energy on activity required for task performance. Thus, through the motivation, facilitation, and constraint of behavior, formal organizational arrangements have a significant potential to influence behavior. When this is combined with the indirect effects of the shaping of individuals and the informal organization, the potential impact is huge, if it is thought through clearly and managed well.

## WHAT DO WE MEAN BY ORGANIZATION DESIGN?

So far, we have used a variety of terms to discuss design. Let us now clarify what is meant by and included in design. When we talk about formal organizational arrangements in the congruence model, we include all of the formal, explicit, and frequently written aspects of organization. Broadly, this includes two types of arrangements: **structures**, or the relatively stable relationships that are specified, and **processes**, or the sequences of steps, series of actions, or methods of operation that are specified. An example of a structure would be the placement of jobs together into a work unit. An example of a process would be a series of steps that a capital spending request must go through for approval.

The congruence model highlights the fact that there may be both formal and informal structures and processes. As we have mentioned, however, the formal structures and processes are much more amenable to direct manipulation.

In this context, our definition of design is as follows:

> Organization design is the making of decisions about the formal organizational arrangements, including the formal structures and the formal processes that make up an organization.

Again, within the context of the congruence model:

> The goal of the organization designer is to develop and implement a set of formal organizational arrangements that will over time

lead to congruence, or good fit, among the different elements of strategy, task, individual, informal organization, and formal organizational arrangements.

While the concepts of structure and process are useful for definition, they are not particularly helpful in making actual design decisions. What do these decisions concretely involve? It is hard to develop an ultimate and all-inclusive list of every possible element, but Figure 3-1 lists the types of design features (both structures and processes) around which managers frequently make decisions. As we think about the case that opened this chapter, we should remember that the division general manager felt that he had finished his design, when in reality, all he had done was to dabble with the first two items on this list.

When we talk about organization design, then, we are talking about managers' decisions about the nature, shape, content, and features of the design elements included in Figure 3-1. To some extent, managers are making design decisions all the time. Every time a specific job is assigned, a procedure created, a method altered, or a job moved, the organization design is being tinkered with. This is not necessarily bad. In fact, one might think about the design's features as tools with which the manager has to work, just as the captain of a sailboat would have such tools as the adjustment of the various sails, rigging, and rudder. The captain is constantly "tuning" his or her boat, even when sailing on a relatively steady course. The effective manager also constantly fine tunes his or her organization design.

There are times, however, when major changes in course are in order. Just as a change in wind and currents or the presence of another boat may require a significant change in how the sailboat is configured, there frequently are times when the manager must make major changes

FIGURE 3-1    What Is Included in Organization Design?

| | |
|---|---|
| 1. Composition of organizational units | |
| 2. Reporting relationships among units | |
| 3. Other structural connections between units | Strategic |
| 4. Organization-wide information, measurement, and control systems | Organization Design |
| 5. Organization-wide methods and procedures | |
| 6. Organization-wide work technologies | |
| | |
| 7. Subunit work resources (tools, materials) | |
| 8. Subunit reward systems | Operational |
| 9. Subunit physical work environment | Design |
| 10. Individual job design | |

in the formal organization and must devote significant attention to making design decisions.

## WHEN TO REDESIGN?

Again, the general organizational model provides a way to determine when significant redesign is required. When the organization evolves to the point at which there are substantial congruence problems between the formal organizational arrangements and the other components, then a redesign should be considered. This is also true prospectively; when an anticipated change will result in problems of fit between the organizational arrangements and one or more of the other components, then a design project should be considered. Specifically, this means that there are a number of situations that might typically justify a significant or systematic redesign of the organization:

1. **Strategic shift:** A major shift in strategy is one situation that frequently requires a redesign. Strategic changes may occur as a result of environmental factors (such as competition, regulation, or new technology), changes in resources, or problems of organizational performance. Such changes may involve a redefinition of the business, the markets, the product-service offerings, or the competitive basis of the organization. These shifts will require individuals in the organization to redirect their efforts and apply resources differently. As a consequence, design changes may be appropriate to ensure that the work is consistent with the new strategy. An example of this comes from Citibank. In the mid-1970s, one of the key strategic objectives of the bank was to develop and maintain banking relationships with large multinational corporations. These corporations could be very good customers for the bank, but competitors also wanted to do business with those same customers. The customers had sophisticated needs and required coordination of service, sometimes on a worldwide basis. In support of the strategic objective, the bank created a new organization, the World Corporate Group, which focused on a particular set of customers. The organization redesign was done in support of a new strategic emphasis.

2. **Task redefinition:** A redesign may also be necessitated by a changing definition of the task. In some cases, as previously described, task redefinition occurs as a result of a strategic shift. However, in other situations, tasks are redefined because of the development of new technologies or changes in the nature, cost,

or quality of available resources. Task changes require people to do things differently. One way to accomplish the change in job performance is through a change in organizational arrangements. A common example of this involves the redesign of organizations that has gone on in many cases as a consequence of the introduction of automated office systems (i.e., word processors, dedicated work stations, local area networks). The new technology has led to a redefinition of the work and thus a restructuring of the organization.

3. **Cultural/political change:** There may be times when a redesign of an organization is required not because of strategic or task considerations, but because key managers want to bring about a shift in the informal organization and choose to use the formal organizational arrangements as a device to achieve this purpose. Sometimes the redesign may be in response to individual needs, such as increased participation in decision making. At other times, it may be directed toward the informal organization itself; making a change in the formal arrangements that the manager predicts will lead to a set of consequences in the informal organization. Many examples of this can be seen in the cases of "new plants" that have been created in the last ten years, particularly in the auto industry. The fundamental objective of these plants (quite a few being redesigns of "old plants") was to create an informal organization characterized by high levels of employee involvement, participation in problem solving, teamwork, and thus high commitment to a quality product. Rarely has one of these plants been created without significant redesign of the formal structures to include such features as fewer levels of hierarchy; wider spans of control; and special employee councils, or steering committees.[1] In fact, to influence a change in the culture or political relationships (the informal organization), significant redesign of the formal organizational arrangements was required.

4. **Growth:** One of the events that commonly leads to redesign is the growth in size and/or scope of an organization. When organizations are relatively small, when most people know each other, and when the relationships are face to face, many of the mechanisms for motivating, facilitating, and constraining behavior can be informal. There is no need to invest time, effort, and energy in the creation of formal arrangements. As an organization (or a part of an organization) grows, however, these informal arrangements may get overloaded or overburdened. As new tasks and strategies are taken on (a natural part of growth), the formal arrangements may no longer be congruent with the rest of the organization. (We will consider this issue in more depth in the

final chapter, with a discussion of how organizations function over time.)

5. **Change in people:** Since effective organizational arrangements are designed with individuals in mind, a change in individuals (either a significant few individuals or a significant change in many individuals) will require a rethinking of the design of the organization. The most graphic examples of this occur through the natural processes of management succession. As a new manager and a new set of players come to lead an organization, the sets of arrangements that fit the needs, skills, talents, and capacities of the previous team may no longer make sense. Similarly, if there are large changes occurring within the work force—changes in needs and preferences, changes in skill levels and education, and/or changes in values—then some rethinking of the organization design may also be in order.

6. **In response to problems with organizational causes:** The cases mentioned so far are largely situations encountered in the normal growth, evolution, and maturation of an organization. Sometimes, however, redesign is necessary because of performance problems that have developed where the causes are organizational (i.e., problems caused by poor organizational fit). What are some symptoms that might indicate the presence of problems with causes related to organization design?

One type of symptom is the presence of difficulties with **coordination,** such as cross-unit projects that do not get done, work units that are uninformed of their responsibilities, and groups that appear to be isolated and out of step with the direction of the rest of the organization. A second, but very much related, symptom is the presence of excessive **conflict** between groups within the organization. Such conflict may be a consequence of poorly or inadequately designed structures or processes. A third symptom is excessive questions about **role clarity**, with individuals or groups being unclear about what is expected of them, about what they are supposed to do, or about where their jobs end and others' begin. Functions may overlap or work may fall "into the cracks" between units. When

FIGURE 3-2     Situations That Frequently Require Redesign

1. Strategic shift
2. Task redefinition
3. Cultural/political change
4. Growth
5. Change in people
6. Problems with existing organization design

roles are unclear, decision making may be tedious, prolonged, and inefficient. Fourth, there are problems of **resource misuse**; resources do not get
to the performers who need them. Specialized functions or individual skills
may not be fully or appropriately utilized. Fifth, there may be disruptions
in the **flow of work** through the organization. Workflows may be too
cumbersome, or there may be foul-ups in moving work through the organization. Sixth is **reduced responsiveness**; somehow, the organization cannot respond appropriately to changes in the environment, to new market
needs, or to product characteristics. In some cases, the organization
responds, but the response is much too late or much too slow. A final
potential symptom is the **proliferation of extraorganizational units**. Where
there is excessive reliance on newly created units (i.e., special task forces,
committees, new units) to do every new piece of work that the organization faces or to deal with every significant challenge, this may indicate that
the basic design is inadequate or that people have so little faith in it that
they will not entrust anything important to be done within the core structures or processes of the organization.

Although these symptoms could reflect a number of problems
with different organizational causes, they frequently indicate an organi-
zation-design-based problem and thus a necessity to at least consider the
option of redesign.

## TYPES OF DESIGN DECISIONS

Once the decision has been made to consider redesign, it is important to collect data to verify that design is indeed a causal factor (see the
problem analysis steps in Chapter 2). It is also important to have a set of
tools and an orderly approach for making design decisions (see Chapters 4 through 8). In this decision-making process, it is helpful to keep in
mind the different types of design decisions that must be made at different times, by different people, and with different criteria.

In the case with which this chapter opened, we saw how the general manager defined his design decisions as the basic unit of composition
and reporting relationships at the top few levels of the organization, and
basically excluded all else. This is natural because it is difficult to think
about all of the different possible design decisions (such as those summarized in Figure 3-1) at the same time. Unfortunately, the typical way of
dealing with this is to focus merely on a few of the boxes and lines at the
top of the organization and to allow the rest to work out somehow.

In practice, two approaches are used in making design decisions.
The first type, **tops-down**, is illustrated by the general manager in this
chapter. The top levels of the organization are the focus, and usually it

is just the unit composition and reporting relationships that take up most of the time and attention. Regardless of how well or how systematically these decisions are made (they were not in our case), a problem results because the rest of the organization frequently is not touched. Thus, while there may be new changes or directions at the top, the rest of the organization is doing the same work, using the same structures and the same processes. In the extreme, we see organizations in which there are periods of constant change at the top with relatively little impact on the rest of the organization.

A second approach is to start with the work being performed at the level of the product or service produced and then to create a design working **bottoms-up**. This approach is advocated by many job design theorists[2] and has been used extensively by internal staff groups within organizations.[3] The work is identified, jobs are built around the work, work flows are constructed, and supervisory and support jobs are created to facilitate the work flow. These are then aggregated again into work units and groups, moving up in the organization. Several problems are frequently encountered with this approach. First, there is an inevitable mismatch at the point where the bottoms-up design meets the top levels of the organization, at which some other design process has been in effect. Where there is conflict, the tops-down perspective usually wins, and therefore many technically excellent designs are never implemented or are planted in hostile ground where they cannot grow, mature, and become truly effective. Bottoms-up designs, because they are not strategic in perspective and are frequently done in a strategic vacuum, may risk making people more effective at performing the wrong tasks.

An insight gained through the authors' work with a corporate organizational design group in AT&T was that neither approach, topsdown nor bottoms-up, was adequate; organization design needs to be done both ways — designing tops-down to implement the strategy, and then, within the context of that design, designing bottoms-up to do the work and to create meaningful and motivating jobs for individuals.

One way of thinking about this is to identify two basic types of design decisions to be made with different criteria, by different people, and at different points in time (see Figure 3-3). Strategic organizational design is driven by strategy and provides the basic shape of the organization for implementing its strategy. Operational organizational design occurs within the context of a strategic design and is driven by current operational concerns, which might vary (for example, cost, quality, meaningful work, or employee involvement).

Organization design is thus seen as bidirectional (see Figure 3-4) with strategic designs (there may be several iterations of strategic design, depending on the size of the organization) working from the top down,

FIGURE 3-3    Strategic and Operational Design

|  | Strategic | Operational |
|---|---|---|
| What Type of Decision | Basic architecture/shape of the organization | Management and operational processes, work flows, jobs, measures |
| What Part of the Organization | Top 2–4 levels | All levels as necessary |
| Direction | Tops-down | Bottoms-up |
| Driven By | Strategy | Operational concerns (cost/quality/time) |

operational designs from the bottom up, and the two meeting usually two or three levels above the actual work performers.

## SUMMARY

**Opening case revisited:**

As we began this chapter, we were in the shoes of the planning director at a large chemical company who was dealing with her boss' design ideas jotted down on a napkin. If we think about this situation in the context of the ideas presented in this chapter, the planning director and the general manager need to have a serious discussion. The first issue is whether there really is a significant need for a new design. There may be, or there may not be. The general manager may simply be looking for something to do to make his mark or to shake things up. Our view is that these do not constitute sufficient reasons for expending the time, effort, and energy involved in an organization redesign activity. If, however, there are substantive reasons to think about redesign, then the planning director will need to work with her boss to determine whether they are talking about a strategic or an operational organization design task. Only then can they think about how they might start to work on the design problem.

In this chapter, we have provided some basic perspectives, concepts, and definitions related to organization design. We have linked design to our general model of organizational performance and discussed what is included in the definition of organizational design. We have iden-

FIGURE 3-4     Tops-Down and Bottoms-Up Design

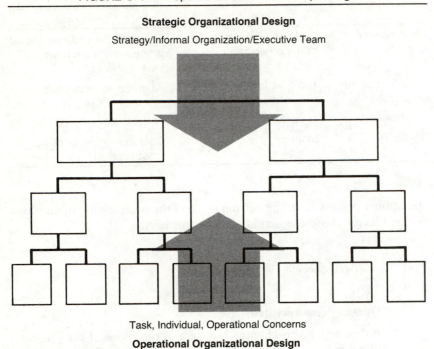

**Strategic Organizational Design**
Strategy/Informal Organization/Executive Team

Task, Individual, Operational Concerns
**Operational Organizational Design**

tified those situations in which significant redesign may be necessary and, in particular, the symptoms that may indicate design problems. Finally, we have provided a way of thinking about the two general types of design decisions — strategic organizational design and operational organization design.

This distinction now provides us with a choice. In this book, we will emphasize strategic design. This does not imply that operational design is not an important, indeed critically significant, part of design decision making. In fact, as we discuss strategic design, we will at many different points refer to related issues of operational design and identify how to make the linkage between the strategic design and the operational design.

The challenge, then, is to figure out how to make key strategic design decisions in an effective manner. One method that is frequently used is trial and error. In practice, managers try different designs by implementing them and seeing how they work. This is a costly, expensive, risky, and ultimately unnecessary approach. We do know enough about organizations and design to work through some of the design options and (at the minimum) eliminate designs that clearly will be less effective or will not work. We can even judge designs and compare their impact before committing to their implementation. This clearly is a more effective approach. However, in order to do this, we need some tools. In the next three chapters, we will provide those tools. In Chapter 4, we will discuss a specific organization design model to help us think about organization design decisions within the context of the more general congruence model. In Chapters 5 and 6, we will examine some of the key decisions in strategic organizational design and discuss some of the alternative options available to managers. In Chapter 7, we will discuss the issues of centralized versus decentralized decision making and managing staff groups within organizations. We will tie all this together in Chapter 8, where we will work through a specific process, or sequence, for making strategic design decisions.

## *NOTES*

1. See, for example: R. Walton, "Innovative Restructuring of Work," in J. Rosow, ed., *The Worker and the Job*, (Englewood Cliffs, NJ: Prentice-Hall, 1974); P. Gyllenhammar, *Dignity at Work*, (Stockholm: Streiffert & Co., 1985); J. O'Toole, et al., *Work in America*, (Cambridge, MA: M.I.T. Press, 1973); M. Hanlon, D. Nadler, and D. Gladstein, *Attempting Work Reform*, (New York: Wiley, 1985).

2. E. Lawler, *Pay and Organization Development*, (Reading, MA: Addison-Wesley, 1981).

3. M. Beer, *Organization Change and Development*, (Santa Monica, CA: Goodyear, 1980); R. Beckhard and R. Harris, *Organizational Transitions*, (Reading, MA: Addison-Wesley, 1977); J. Galbraith, *Designing Complex Organizations*, (Reading, MA: Addison-Wesley, 1973); R. Kilman and W. McKelvey, "Organization Design: A Participative Multivariate Approach," *Administrative Science Quarterly* 20 (1975): 24–36.

# 4

# A Conceptual Model for Thinking About Design Decisions

**Case:**

High Technology Products Inc. (HTP) has long been a leader in the field of electronic products for office use. It has built its leadership on product innovation. Through smart investments in research and technology, it has become known as the innovator in its particular industry segment, and HTP products have long been seen as the standard by which other products are assessed. For many years, in fact, HTP has developed and maintained such a significant lead in basic technology (protected by patents in some cases) that it has been able to sell new products simply on the basis of one-page product announcements. Customers would willingly wait months and pay a premium for an HTP product because it was uniquely state of the art.

While the company has moved into a number of areas of activity, the heart of the business is the Advanced Products Group (see Figure 4-1), headed by Sam Tucker, an executive vice-president, who serves as the group head. Reporting to the group head are four vice-presidents, each heading a major division. The Research Division is responsible for basic research in electronics and other disciplines relevant to the HTP product line. The Product Development and Engineering Division is responsible for developing the work of the Research Division, where possible, into applications, features, or whole products. The result of their work should be a product that is ready to be manufactured and

FIGURE 4-1     High Technology Products Inc. (HTP) Organization Chart

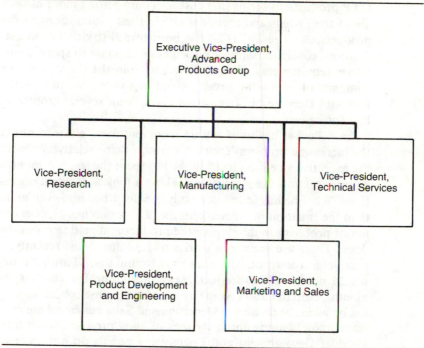

sold. The Manufacturing Division is responsible for production of the product, including preproduction engineering, purchasing, and distribution. The Marketing and Sales Division is responsible for selling HTP products, primarily through a small but technically well-versed direct sales force. Finally, the Technical Service Division is responsible for installation, maintenance, and some limited customer support in the field.

During the last five years, and in the most recent two years in particular, HTP has experienced some difficult times. The maturing of some of the product lines has resulted in HTP's losing a good deal of its competitive edge. New competition has also entered the scene—some very tough foreign competitors in particular. In other product areas, there has been a faster rate of change so that HTP has found itself either "with the pack" or behind, rather than in a commanding position. Finally, customers seem to be demanding more. They want more support in using HTP products, they seem to be less patient, and they are less willing to pay a premium now that they see competitive products that are comparable but significantly less expensive. In addition, customers have been complaining more about quality problems in HTP products. It seems that customers are getting more explicit about their needs and more definite in their expectations of the products. As a result, HTP has been forced to develop special features, configurations, or packages in response to specific customer requirements. This is different from the days when the company offered a few products and customers had to be satisfied with them and in fact, often had to wait several months in line for delivery.

Sam Tucker has been getting more and more alarmed about the increasing problems facing his group. Being relatively new in the executive vice-president job, he has spent the last few months getting to know the market and taking a look at internal operations. What he has found internally has disturbed him even more than the situation in the marketplace. The group has experienced major problems in developing the product and getting it out the door. There are numerous stories of foul-ups. Most recently, a product introduction was made only to find that Manufacturing would not have the product ready in volume for another six months. Sam has also become aware of the intense conflicts brewing between the divisions. Marketing and Sales personnel are constantly complaining about the lack of good product, about how Product Development and Engineering people do not seem to want to talk to them about customer needs and the competition, and about scheduling and distribution problems from the factories. The Manufacturing people have complained that Marketing and Sales people are unrealistic in their expectations, and the Product Development Division has argued that if they listen to the Marketing and Sales Division and copy every low-budget innovation that cheap competitors are introducing, they will continue to fritter away the HTP technological lead and reputation. Meanwhile, the Technical Service Division has been complaining about the increasing number of machine failures in the field and the amount of time that they must spend making design changes in the field as a result of Engineering change orders. Finally, Tucker had just been out to the Research Division headquarters to hear a presentation on the increasing turnover rate among technical personnel and scientists who seem to be frustrated by how few of their ideas and innovations are getting into the products.

After thinking about the events inside the company during the past year, Tucker was amazed to learn that things were much worse in the marketplace. He was beginning to think that maybe it was time to restructure the organization, to redesign it from the ground up to somehow do a better job. He felt that the basic pieces were still in place—their technology was good, the people were excellent, the name was still very good, and the product strategy was fundamentally sound. Something was preventing his group's making it all work.

## INTRODUCTION

Sam Tucker has discovered that he may have an organization design problem. While he seems to have the basic elements of an effective strategy and his people are good, something is getting in the way of its all coming together. The symptoms he observes seem to indicate that at least part of the problem may be related to organization design. It appears that the organizational arrangements that used to be congruent with the strategy and the work no longer fit.

Sam now needs to identify the element in the organization that does not fit. To do so, he needs to go beyond the general concepts of congruence and organizational systems and use some more specific tools for looking at the effectiveness of various organization designs in performing different kinds of work. He needs help both in diagnosing the specific problems with his current design and in developing a new design that will help fix his problems.

In this chapter, we will explore a conceptual model for thinking about organization design decisions. In the first section of the chapter, we will provide a brief background about different ways of thinking about design decisions and then, in the second section, discuss the specific model that we will use in subsequent chapters.

## BACKGROUND—APPROACHES TO DESIGN DECISION MAKING

The search for models to help managers make organization design decisions has been going on for centuries. It is only in the last one hundred years, however, that significant attempts have been made to write about generalized rules for designing organizations.

In the late nineteenth and early twentieth centuries, most writers on organization were searching for a set of universal design principles. They were looking for the "one best way" to structure an organization. They developed models composed of sets of rules (for example, the ideal span of control is six subordinates) that managers could use in structuring organizations. The general bias of these rules was that organizations would work better when there were highly formalized and rational procedures, rules, and methods; when jobs were designed to be simple (so people could be interchangeable); and when decision making occurred at the top of the organization and people at the bottom carried out those decisions according to the rules. These principles-of-management writers focused on the formal aspects of organizations, and their underlying model was one of a machine.[1] If the right working parts could be designed and produced to specification, then the machine would work. In terms of our congruence perspective, these writers focused almost single-mindedly on the task-organizational arrangements fit and were aiming to identify universally applicable formulas for designing organizations that would fit any task.

In the late 1940s and through the 1960s, a second approach became popular. This approach rightfully criticized the classical management theorists for failing to consider what we would call the individual and informal organization elements of organizational life. These theorists advocated creating organizations that were much less formal and in which decision making was widely shared, communication and information flowed freely, and people at the bottom of the organization had a lot of say about how things were done.[2] These later theorists were similar to the earlier theorists in that they also saw this approach as universal. They were also prescribing the one best way to organize in all situations.

Starting in 1960 and continuing through the 1970s, a third approach emerged.[3] This approach stemmed from empirical research to determine if, in reality, there was any relationship between an organization's design and its effectiveness. The researchers found such a relationship, but over time they saw a pattern that was significantly different than either of the earlier approaches. They found that different situations seemed to require different types of designs. Rather than finding a universal approach, they discovered that the decision about what type of design is most effective is contingent on a number of factors that vary from situation to situation. Thus, this approach has been called the **contingency approach** because it moves away from the idea of one best way to design organizations. These researchers struggled for a long time to find the right set of factors and to develop some decision rules to help identify which kinds of designs to use in particular situations. They tried various approaches. Some research seemed to indicate that the most effective type of design is contingent on the technology involved. Other researchers looked to the environment, while still others looked at the work process or task itself.

In the early 1970s, design theorist Jay Galbraith proposed a concept that seemed to integrate many of the different contingency approaches.[4] He proposed that if one thought about organizations as information-processing systems — mechanisms that moved information to people so they could do their work and accomplish tasks—it would be possible to develop some general rules for thinking about the contingencies of design. While the debate about design continues and the research work goes on, this information-processing theory has turned out to be relatively useful in making design decisions and has received considerable acceptance in both academic and managerial circles. It is also very consistent with open-systems views of organizations. We will therefore be using it here as the basis of our design model.

## AN INFORMATION-PROCESSING MODEL FOR ORGANIZATION DESIGN

In this model, the fundamental function of organizational arrangements is to process information. Most of what moves around organizations is information—information about markets, information about behavior, instructions and rules, and measures of performance. A set of organization arrangements collects and channels information to individuals and groups in support of the work they do. Therefore, the key to fit is to match the information-processing capacities of the organization design to the information-movement or -processing requirements of the work. We can think about this in terms of three basic propositions that make up the model.

1. **Different tasks pose different information-processing requirements.**

Different types of work require different patterns of information movement in order for the work to get done. This can best be illustrated by example. In Figure 4-2, we have used the HTP case to portray two types of task situations and to compare the information-movement requirements in each task.

Scenario 1 describes the old strategy and work situation that used to exist at HTP. Prior to the changes in competition, customers, and technology, the task of the Advanced Products Group in HTP was relatively straightforward. The whole group was charged with developing technologically sophisticated and innovative products, which could be produced and sold to customers. In this scenario, the Research Division focused on basic investigation. When they found something with potential applications, they passed it on to the Product Development Division, which in turn transformed the technology into a product and then passed it on to Manufacturing, who figured out how to build it. Once the product was in production, Marketing and Sales introduced it to customers. After the

FIGURE 4-2    HTP Information-Processing Requirements: Two Task Scenarios

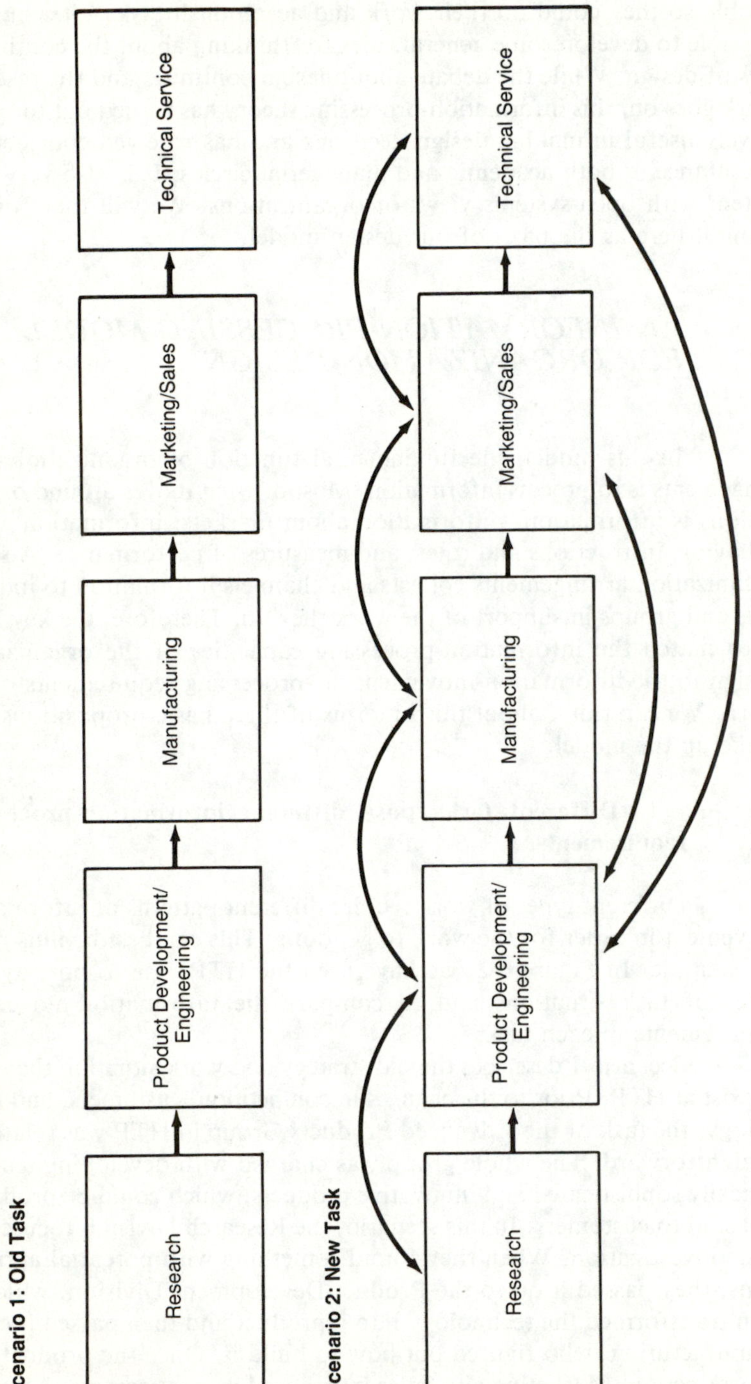

**Scenario 1: Old Task**

**Scenario 2: New Task**

completion of sales, the Technical Service Division provided support in the field.

In Figure 4-2, we have outlined the required flow of information among the various units in order to get the work done. It is fairly simple and straightforward. For example, once Product Development receives information about the new technology from Research, they no longer need much contact with that division. Similarly, once they hand off a product to Manufacturing, they are done with it. The movement of information required to do the work is simply a set of serial hand offs down the line between the divisions—a straightforward "bucket brigade" of information.

Now let us look at a different situation. The bottom diagram in Figure 4-2 describes the current information flow required to perform the tasks facing the Advance Products Group. Because of competition, the loss of a commanding technological lead, and new customer demands, the tasks of product development, manufacturing, and marketing are different than they were before. Rather than develop products in a comfortable vacuum, the Product Development Division needs to be in contact with the Marketing people to understand the changing requirements and customer demands. They also need to know what products and services competitors are offering. Because of price competition, they need to work with Manufacturing to see if the product can be made at a reasonable unit manufacturing cost. They also need information from Technical Service about the performance of the products in the field and the types of problems and concerns that customers have with the equipment in use. Due to an ever dynamic marketplace (competition does not stand still), this exchange of information has to be conducted continually. Since pressures are exerted by competitors in the form of new product introductions and short delivery times, the divisions must exchange information at a much quicker pace than they ever did before. Thus, the amount of information that must now move among the divisions in order to perform a task is much greater. Information exchange must occur more frequently, must be done more quickly, and is much more complex. The demands of the work (the task) have changed.

How do these two task scenarios differ, and why do they require different patterns of information movement? Some of the key factors differentiating these tasks are outlined in Figure 4-3. The tasks are different in three key dimensions. First, the tasks vary in their **predictability**. Formerly, HTP dictated the customer requirements, and so, when new products were developed, it was easy to predict customer response. In fact, very little happened that HTP did not already know about. In this new situation, many things occur that HTP cannot predict, and thus HTP must react to and process new information much more frequently. Second, the tasks vary in the degree to which they are **environmentally impacted**. When HTP controlled the technology and there were few com-

FIGURE 4-3     Tasks and Information-Processing Requirements

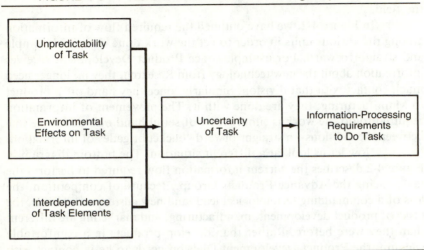

petitors, little that occurred in the outside world was of consequence to HTP. Now, information about competitors or new technologies is needed to do the task of product development. Without that information, HTP runs the risk of developing a product that is not competitive or is not state-of-the-art. Third, the tasks vary in the degree of **interdependence of the task elements**. When HTP was developing a few standard products, each division was minimally dependent on the others to do its work. Once a division finished its work on a product, it could hand it off to another. When the task matured to one of responsiveness to changing and unique customer needs, the divisions suddenly became more intensely dependent on one another. Product Development depends on Marketing to provide competitive intelligence and information on changing customer needs; conversely, Marketing is dependent on Product Development and Manufacturing to modify product features and production schedules to enable Technical Service to promise competitive features and delivery times. A host of additional interdependences now exist that did not exist before.

What is important is the consequence of these changes to the tasks to be performed. Those who have observed and measured work have noted that as the unpredictability of the task, the instability of the environment, and the interdependence of tasks increase, the degree of uncertainty involved in doing the work also increases significantly. Uncertainty is a lack of information about what will occur. Since the future becomes less certain and less predictable, there is more of a need to move information quickly to those who need it. There is an increased need to exchange information in order to coordinate efforts and to make necessary adjustments to changes. Therefore, different types of tasks present different types and amounts of information-processing requirements.

    **2. Different organization designs provide different types of information-processing capacity.**

    Just as tasks vary in the information-processing requirements they pose, organization designs vary in their capacity to process information. Structures and processes facilitate the movement of information in various ways. Specifically, three elements of organization design seem to play a major role in determining how information is moved (see Figure 4-4).

    **Grouping** involves the aggregation of work functions, positions, and individuals into work units. Grouping takes place whenever a structure is created involving units, departments, divisions, groups, or even whole companies within larger holding companies. Grouping explicitly puts some jobs (and thus people) together into the same units and implicitly separates some jobs and people. This is unavoidable. Each time jobs or units are put together in a group, they are separated from others. Grouping impacts greatly on what information is processed to whom because it is much more difficult to move information across the boundaries of groups than within groups. The natural tendency of groups to move toward their own views of the world (and, in the extreme, toward conflict) makes it more difficult to move information to other groups. In

FIGURE 4-4    Structure and Information-Processing Capacity

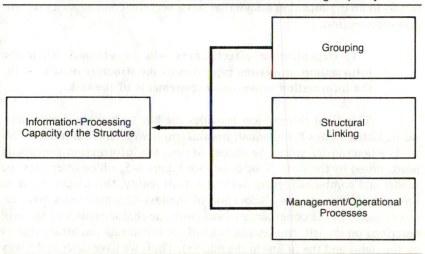

HTP, the basic grouping reflected in the structure of the divisions makes it difficult to move the information that is needed to do the task described in the second scenario.

A second element of design that affects information flow is **structural linking**. Structural linking involves the creation of formal connections (relationships) between different groups. The most common way of connecting groups is through the hierarchy, for example, by having two groups report to the same manager (thus becoming two units in a larger, higher-level group). There are, however, many other ways of linking groups structurally, such as cross-unit groups, integrators, and planning teams. The point is that the creation of structural links facilitates the movement of information among the groups that are linked and thus varies the information-processing capacity of the whole system. For example, if product teams were created that crossed the boundaries of the five divisions in HTP, it might improve the ability of the design to move information among the groups as needed.

Third, various **management and operational processes**, such as information systems, control systems, goals, meetings, and rewards systems are designed around the groups and structural linking devices. These processes facilitate the movement and processing of information and thus support information movement among the groups. In HTP, project review processes, or meetings, and special accelerated product planning and development processes are examples of the kind of design device that could be used to enhance the movement of information through the system.

The key point to keep in mind is that each combination of grouping, structural linking, and management/operational process decisions results in an organization design that has a very different capacity to process information.

**3. Organization effectiveness will be greatest when the information-processing capacities of the structure match, or fit, the information-processing requirements of the task.**

This final proposition provides the key to making design decisions. Other things being equal, organizations will function more effectively when the design can be shaped to meet the information-processing needs posed by the work to be done. See Figure 4-5, which integrates the model and combines Figures 4-3 and 4-4. In reality, this diagram can be thought of as merely an elaboration of the task-organizational arrangements pieces of the congruence model (with the characteristics of the task described on the left, the key elements of the organizational arrangements on the right, and the fit line in the middle). Thus, we have described a way of looking at fit in more concrete and observable terms.

FIGURE 4-5    The Information-Processing Model

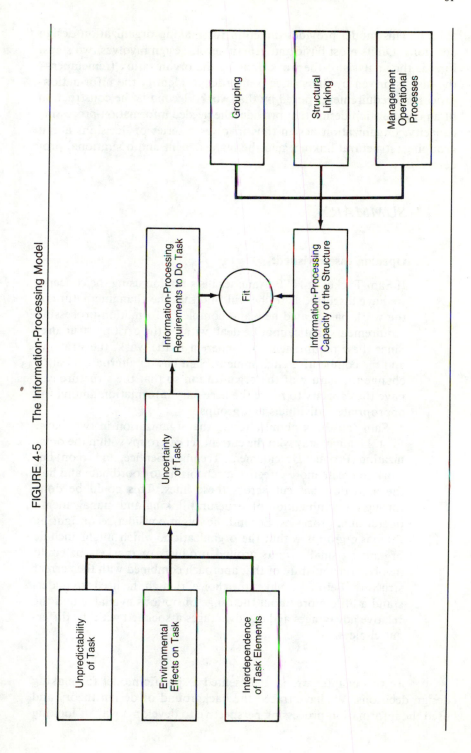

This model provides direction for making organization design decisions. On its most basic and general level, design involves two steps. First is the analysis of the work done by the organization (remember — the task is driven by the strategy) in order to identify the information-processing requirements posed by that work. Second is the construction of an organization design that provides the needed information-processing capacity. Organization design thus involves a series of decisions about grouping, structural linking, and the management and operational processes.

## SUMMARY

**Opening case revisited:**

If Sam Tucker at HTP examines his situation using the concepts we have discussed here, he will find that the changing nature of the work has created new and complex information-processing requirements that cannot be dealt with by the existing structure. Since these requirements are inherent in the work, the strategy, and the competitive environment, Sam has no alternative but to change the nature of the organization so that the structure can have the capacity to move the necessary information among the appropriate individuals and groups.

Sam can think about altering the organization in two ways. First, he might stay with the current set of groups within the organization (Product Development, Technical Service, and so on) but work to create more effective mechanisms to coordinate and link the activities that cut across these lines. This could be done through a combination of structural linking and management/operational processes. Second, he might consider reconfiguring the basic groups within the organization, which might include organizing smaller units around products or markets or could involve some mixture of that approach combined with the current structure. Before he makes the choice, though, he needs to understand a little more about the range of options available and the relative advantages and disadvantages associated with the different choices.

In this chapter we have presented a specific model for making design decisions. We have traced the background of design theory and used the information-processing perspective to develop a way of looking at work, at organization design, and finally, at the relationship between them. We are moving toward the application of the model in a sequence of design decisions, which starts with analysis of the strategy and work and moves toward making specific design decisions. First, however, we will look at some of the specific options available to the designer when making decisions about grouping, structural linking, and management/operational processes.

## NOTES

1. For a review, see J. Maisse, "Management Theory," in J. March, ed., *Handbook of Organizations*, (Chicago: Rand McNally, 1965); H. Koontz, ed., *Toward a Unified Theory of Management*, (New York: McGraw-Hill, 1964).

2. C. Argyris, *Interpersonal Competence and Organization Effectiveness*, (Homewood, IL: Irwin, 1962); R. Likert, *New Patterns of Management*, (New York: McGraw-Hill, 1961); W. Bennis, *Changing Organizations: Essays on the Development and Evolution of Human Organization*, (New York: McGraw-Hill, 1967); W. Burke, *Organization Development*, (Boston, MA: Little, Brown, 1982); C. Perrow, *Complex Organizations*, (Glenview, IL: Scott, Foresman, 1972).

3. R. Lawrence and J. Lorsch, *Organization and Environment*, (Cambridge, MA: Harvard University Press, 1967); J. Woodward, *Industrial Organization*, (New York: Oxford University Press, 1965); J. Thompson, *Organizations in Actions*, (New York: McGraw-Hill, 1967).

4. J. Galbraith, *Designing Complex Organizations*, (Reading, MA: Addison-Wesley, 1973); M. Tushman and D. Nadler, "Information Processing as an Integrating Concept in Organization Design," *Academy of Management Review* 3 (1978): 613–24; A. Van de Ven and R. Drazin, "The Concept of Fit in Contingency Theory," in B. Staw and L. Cummings, eds., *Research in Organization Behavior*, (Greenwich, CT: JAI Press, 1985); for a thorough review on organization design, see P. Nystrom and W. Starbuck, *Handbook of Organization Design*, (New York: Oxford University Press, 1981).

# 5

# Choosing the Basic Architecture of the Organization: Strategic Grouping

**Case:**

John Torrence, Senior Vice-President of R&D, was puzzled by the lack of new product development at Medtek. Of more direct concern was the performance of the R&D facility. While widely recognized as employing top-flight scientists and engineers, the laboratory was rife with conflict, low morale, and poor individual and organization productivity. Torrence's laboratory was organized by disciplinary area (see Figure 5-1). While this seemed to encourage excellence in the respective areas, it did not help in the coordination of product development efforts. New product development efforts were plagued with quality, reliability, and cost problems. As part of his comprehensive effort in organization renewal, Torrence was weighing the costs and benefits of moving to a program structure in his laboratory. Or, should he adapt a matrix structure that had just been implemented by a competitor? Further, given the lack of effective coordination between Research and Advanced Development and the similarity in their work, Torrence was considering combining these units into a single laboratory area.

John Torrence is grappling with the most fundamental questions in organization design: (1) should the laboratory adopt a disciplinary, product, or matrix structure and (2) how specialized should he focus the

FIGURE 5-1    Medtek Corporation Organization Chart

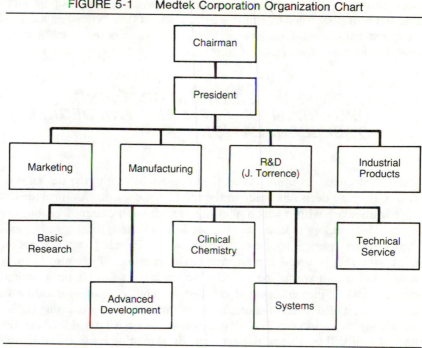

laboratory. All of Torrence's other design decisions (that is, linking and operational design) will hinge on the laboratory's basic structural architecture. While Torrence grapples with these issues, the choices involved in strategic grouping are the initial choices in any organization design problem. This chapter discusses the issues of strategic grouping; we lay out the grouping options, discuss their strengths and weaknesses, and link strategic grouping to business unit strategy and information-processing demands.

Organization design is the allocation of scarce resources (people, budgets, space) to achieve a specified purpose. Organization design, at its core, involves choices as to grouping some resources in order to gain economies of scale, benefits of specialization, and/or integration. However, once resources are specialized, the complementary aspect of organization design is to provide those structural linking mechanisms to help knit interdependent areas together. For example, in the Medtek example, Torrence could choose to structure the laboratory in a disciplinary, product, matrix, or mixed form. Each structure has its own strengths and weaknesses. Whatever his choice, Torrence needs to complement his *grouping* choice with the appropriate set of *linking* mechanisms. Strategic design involves these two core sets of decisions. Strategic grouping involves grouping some resources together (thereby splitting some resources) and choosing a degree of specialization. Strategic linking, the second decision set, involves coordinating groups together (see Chapter 6).

## CHOICES IN STRATEGIC GROUPING: ORGANIZATION FORM AND THE DEGREE OF SPECIALIZATION

Strategic grouping is the most important step in the design process. Grouping decisions made at the top of the organization provide the core framework within which all other organization design decisions are made. Grouping puts some tasks, functions, or disciplines together and draws others apart; it focuses the organization. People grouped together are better able to discuss, plan, and perform a task. They also become more skilled and specialized as they dedicate their efforts on a limited range of tasks. Since grouping affects people's ability to communicate with each other, it also affects the organization's information-processing capacity. Grouping decisions affect what the organization will be able to do well and what it will be able to do less well. By providing basic coordination through common supervision, resources, and systems, grouping decisions give shape to what and how work gets done.[1]

Strategic grouping involves two related subdecisions: (1) what is the basic form of the organization and (2) given the organization's form, how specialized or differentiated are organizational components. For example, at Medtek, Torrence must decide (1) between the disciplinary, project, and matrix forms for the laboratory and (2) given his choice of one of these forms, how specialized should the units be. Should he split basic research from advanced development in his disciplinary organization, or if he chooses a project organization, should this organization be split in two, three, or four product areas?

The initial choice in strategic grouping (that of core organization form) flows directly from the organization's or unit's strategy. Certain organization forms will more effectively accomplish certain strategies. Management needs to choose the strategic form that best meets strategic contingencies. The second choice in strategic grouping, choosing the degree of specialization, hinges on the unit's work-related uncertainty. Those units facing complex and/or heterogeneous task environments or facing complex, highly specialized task requirements will need more specialized organization forms. For example, if Torrence wants to do both basic research and more local problem-solving work in his laboratory, and if the rate of change in technology is substantial, he will have to separate basic research from advanced development in order to effectively accomplish both kinds of work.

As with choices of linking (Chapter 6) and managing culture (Chapter 8), the issue of strategic grouping is not just for senior managers. Rather, strategic grouping decisions must be made in a coordinated fashion at multiple levels in an organization. For example, at Medtek, strategic grouping decisions have to be made by Medtek's president as well as by managers of areas that report to Torrence. The issue of strategic grouping is, then, the initial problem to be confronted by *any* manager considering the question of organization design. We discuss the choices of organization form and degree of specialization in greater detail in the next section.

## STRATEGIC GROUPING: CHOICE OF ORGANIZATION FORM

Independent of level in the hierarchy, there is a limited set of organization form options. Each option focuses the organization or unit in a different fashion. Organizations can be organized by activity, output, user/customer, or any combination of these options. While these generic types seldom exist in pure form, they do represent the set of options from which managers choose (see Figure 5-2).

### Organization form options

*Grouping by activity* • **Grouping by activity** puts individuals to work on the same functions, discipline, skills, or work process together. For example, in functional organizations, individuals who perform the same function or skill are grouped together. Grouping by activity can also include grouping by knowledge, skill, and/or discipline. For example, those who assemble are grouped together and are thus separate from those who design; chemists are grouped together and thus separate from biologists; and Manufacturing is grouped separately from Sales (see Figure 5-3). For example, prior to its breakup, AT&T was an enormous functional organization at the corporate level and within the operating companies (see Figure 5-4).

Grouping by activity also applies to the criterion of time. Individuals who are working on projects with short time frames might be grouped together, and those working with long time frames might be grouped together. For example, short-range planners would be grouped separately from long-range planners. Also, when designing a division that

FIGURE 5-2    Organization Form Options

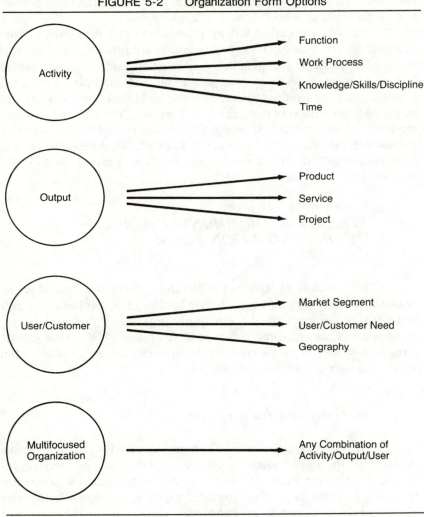

functions twenty-four hours a day, it may be appropriate to group according to shifts, as in a nursing department, where management must be designated for first, second, and third shifts. In activity-dominated organizations, functional/disciplinary/activity goals are emphasized; influence is through functional/disciplinary/activity managers; and rewards and controls are driven by functional or activity considerations.

*Grouping by output* • When grouping by output, people are grouped together on the basis of the *service* or *product* they provide. The people within each group perform different activities, but they are all con-

FIGURE 5-3     Grouping by Activity

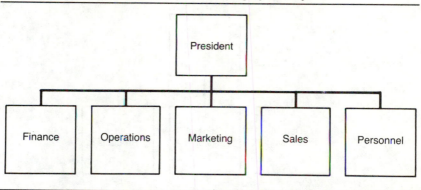

FIGURE 5-4     AT&T (Pre-Breakup)

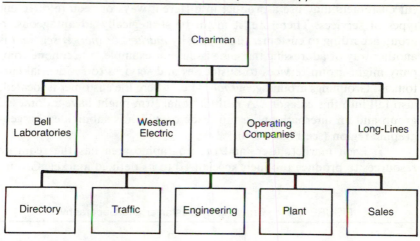

tributors to the same output. A classic illustration is the product organization. In a business equipment firm, for example, product groupings might include Data Processing, General Systems, and Office Products (see Figure 5-5). For example, Volvo organizes its transportation business by truck and automobiles.

Within each output area there are requisite resources to produce the product, service, or project. In output-focused organizations, product, service, or output goals are emphasized; influence is dominated by those concerned with output integrity; and rewards, promotion, and controls are dominated by product, project, and/or service considerations.

FIGURE 5-5    Grouping by Output

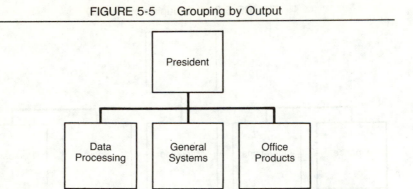

*Grouping by user or customer* • People who are performing different activities and producing different output might be grouped together because they all service the same *user, customer,* or *client.* Different customers may use a product in different ways or require different types of services. Therefore, it might be strategically advantageous to group according to customer. Grouping by *markets* or *market segment* is another way of addressing the same issue. For example, a telephone company might group services to businesses and services to residential customers. Groupings around *geography*, i.e., where the customer is located, also fall into this category. A multinational firm might have a domestic group and an international group, each of which is subdivided by geographic region (see Figure 5-6).

Each market, user, and/or geographic area has the requisite resources to produce products specialized to its defined market. Group-

FIGURE 5-6    Grouping by Customer and Geography

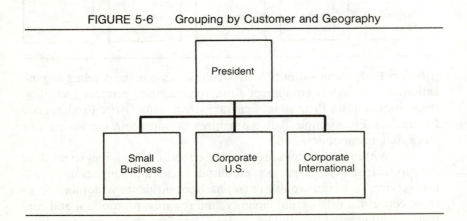

ing by user or client focuses the unit on user/market/geographic consider-ations. User goals are emphasized, influence is dominated by those concerned with user needs, and rewards and controls are dominated by user dimensions of merit.

*Grouping by multiple foci* • Some competitive environments or organization strategies require focus along *several dimensions simultaneously*. For example, at Medtek, Torrence might choose to organize the laboratory by product *and* by discipline. In this fashion, the laboratory could maximize disciplinary competence as well as product integrity. Multifocused organizations can be organized along any set of competitive dimensions. Many multinational organizations are organized by country (i.e., geography) *and* by product provided (commercial, corporate, retail [see Figure 5-7]). For example, during the 1970s Corning Glass Works was organized by product and by geography (see Figure 5-8).

Organizations with multiple foci (sometimes labeled "matrix organizations") attempt to maximize several strategic considerations simultaneously. In a product/geography matrix, for example, there is an emphasis on multiple objectives (e.g,. in product and geography), and influence must be shared by those representing product issues and those representing geographic considerations. Reward, control, and measurement systems must be developed to assess performance along each strategic dimension. We will discuss this form of organization in greater detail in Chapter 6.

FIGURE 5-7    Grouping by Multiple Foci: Matrix Organizations

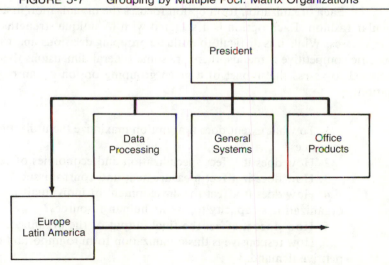

FIGURE 5-8    Corning Glass Works (1978)

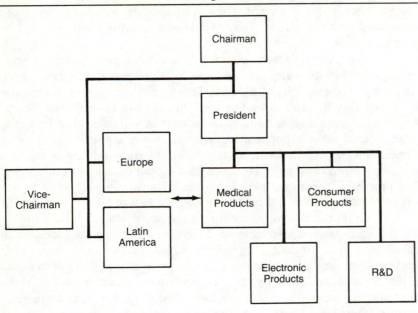

## Consequences of organization form options

Each organization form option focuses the organization in a particular fashion. Each option is associated with its unique strengths and weaknesses. While it is difficult to evaluate grouping decisions apart from specific competitive demands, there are some general dimensions that can be used to assess the impact of a given grouping option on an organization:

1. To what extent does that option maximize the utilization of resources?

2. How does it affect specialization and economies of scale?

3. How does it affect measurement and control issues?

4. How does it affect the development of individuals and the organization's capacity to use its human resources?

5. How does it affect the final output of the organization?

6. How responsive is this organization form to important competitive demands?

*Utilization of resources*  •  Grouping by activity maximizes the utilization of resources because individuals performing the same function or activity can share resources, develop specialized capabilities, and develop a relatively large critical mass of expertise. For example, chemists, if grouped together, can develop a large critical mass and gain the benefits of diverse professional exposure. When grouping by output, by user/client or geography, resources must be duplicated. Human and physical resources must be specialized by product, market, or geography. For example, in a product organization, each product division would require its own manufacturing, development, and marketing departments.

*Specialization and economies of scale*  •  When individuals are grouped by activity, they gain the benefits of a larger critical mass as well as the ability to specialize in a professionally relevant fashion. For example, chemists might specialize in physical chemistry. This combination of large critical mass and activity-based specialization permits increased economies of scale as activity-focused areas perform the same functions repeatedly. The benefits of scale economies diminish, however, when a functional group becomes so large that it begins to incur the expenses of increased bureaucracy, extensive support staff, and increased organizational inertia.

Grouping by output or user/client dedicates resources to focused areas. Individuals do not specialize by activity/discipline but by product, market, or output. Thus, in the chemistry example, chemists in a product organization would focus their energies on some particular product and/or market area. Output/user organizations will not have the economies of scale and will not have large professional reference groups, but they will dedicate more limited resources to focused products and/or markets. Where activity-based units have scale economies and critical mass, output- and user-based units dedicate a more limited, more specialized resource set to focused products, markets, or geographies.

*Measurement and control issues*  •  Grouping by activity, output, or user/customer focuses the firm's resources and affects what is evaluated and measured. If individuals are grouped by function, it is easier to develop standards for performance and to measure and control individuals or groups along functional, disciplinary, or work dimensions. That is, how good is this person's chemistry, what is the quality of the marketing research? In output-focused organizations, it is comparatively easier to monitor the quantity and quality of output. That is, how good is this person's chemistry work for this client set? In user/client strategic groups, then, the measurement and control system addresses the unique needs of the served market. In each case, there are trade-offs in the measurement and control systems. As these systems are dedicated to users, markets, and/or functions, they pay relatively less attention to other dimensions of merit. Multifocused organizations attempt to build measurement and control systems to track multiple dimensions simultaneously.

*Human resources* • Grouping by activity fosters the development of professional identity and skills as individuals become experts at general functions or disciplines. As this specialization increases, individuals risk becoming more narrow in their organizational perspective, and the likelihood of conflict between specialized groups increases. On the other hand, in output or user/client groupings, individuals have less of an opportunity to specialize by function or activity, but a much greater opportunity to work with specialists from other areas in the firm. This focus on markets and/or users increases an individual's exposure to multifunctional or general management issues, yet at the cost of possible disciplinary or functional obsolescence. Thus, a clear human resource trade-off is again one of specialization by activity/profession versus specialization by product and/or market. Thus, a chemist in a disciplinary laboratory is likely to identify with other chemists in the firm. However, a chemist in the industrial products area is likely to identify with industrial product chemists and with other professionals concerned with the delivery of industrial products.

*Organization outputs* • Grouping decisions focus the firm; different organization forms attend to fundamentally different outputs. Grouping by activity creates specialists and relatively large areas of functional, disciplinary, and/or skill excellence, which needs to be integrated to produce a final product or service. Grouping by activity gains disciplinary and work excellence at the expense of integration. Grouping by output facilitates integration by product and product innovation. Grouping by client/user enables the organization to be more responsive to client needs, to cross-sell products, and to reduce duplication in the marketplace.

Activity-based organizations encourage innovation within a discipline or function, where market/user/client organization facilitates innovation to served markets or product areas. Similarly, activity-based organizations respond rapidly to functional or disciplinary considerations but less rapidly to product or market demands. On the other hand, market and product organizations are very responsive to the served market but less so to underlying disciplines or functional innovation. Multifocused organizations attempt to balance these multiple considerations simultaneously.

There is, then, no ideal choice of organizational forms. Each strategic grouping option is associated with its own set of strengths and weaknesses (see Figure 5-9). Most broadly, activity-based organizations buy scale economies and functional excellence at the cost of integration. These forms tend to be innovative in technologies or functions but less responsive to markets, users, and clients. Output and user/client forms buy integration at the cost of specialization. These organizational forms attend to

| FIGURE 5-9 | Consequences of Grouping Options | | |
|---|---|---|---|
| **Organization Form** | | | |
| Activity (Functional/Discipline) | Output (Product/ Service) | User (Market, Geography) | Multifocused (Product/Market, etc.) |
| *Benefits:*<br>— Colleagueship for technical specialists<br>— Supports substantial critical mass by function/discipline | *Benefits:*<br>— High product, service, market, or geographic visibility<br>— Focused coordination by product, service, market, or geography<br>— Relatively easy cross-functional communication | | *Benefits*<br>— Focused attention to multiple objectives<br>— Coordination and specialization |
| *Costs:*<br>— Poor inter-unit coordination<br>— Decisions pile at top<br>— Restricted view of whole | *Costs:*<br>— Duplication of resources<br>— Lose critical mass, specialization by function, discipline<br>— Difficult to allocate pooled resources | | *Costs:*<br>— Substantial conflict<br>— Costly to implement and design<br>— Highly unstable |

Source: R. Duncan, "What Is the Right Organization Structure?" *Organization Dynamics* (Winter 1979).

served markets and product areas yet are less responsive to fundamental changes in underlying disciplinary or functional areas. Multifocused organizations attempt to gain the benefits of several types of strategic grouping. As we will see in Chapter 6, however, the benefits of multifocused organizations must be weighed against the cost of implementing and managing their more complex structures, systems, and cultures.

## Making organization form decisions

There is no optimal organization form; each has its own strengths and weaknesses. How, then, does a manager or a group of managers make the decision about organization form? The most central function of an organization's structure is to help the organization attend to and deal with critical contingencies, and the primary factor in choosing organization form is an organization's or unit's strategy.

At the organization level of analysis, the choice of form should be based on critical strategic contingencies and key success factors. *Strat-*

*egy needs to drive the choice of organization form.* For example, between 1913 and the mid-1970s, AT&T's strategy was one of low-cost, universal service. This strategy was effectively accomplished with an enormous functional organization. However, as competitive and legal conditions changed, and AT&T's strategy had to encompass unregulated business and regulated residential markets, so too did the structure of the operating groups change. During the late 1970s, the operating companies' structures moved to a *market focus*; that is, they dedicated focused resources to business areas and other focused resources to residential customers.

The organization's strategy should set the focus for all grouping decisions. Strategy should be derived from an assessment of competitive environments, organizational resources, and the firm's unique history (see Chapter 2). Strategy sets organizational priorities and dictates which issues and concerns need to be managed most closely. For example, if markets are uncertain, competition stiff, and fundamentally different client needs are identified, one might organize around users/clients. If, on the other hand, innovation in certain product niches is of utmost concern, then it might be most effective to organize around output. If the most pressing strategic issues are cost and efficiency, then grouping by activity or function might be most appropriate. For any one strategy, management must weigh the strengths and weaknesses of the several choices of organization form and choose that organizational form option that is most congruent with the firm's strategy.

At the subunit level, choice of unit form must be driven by business unit or functional strategy and/or by unit objectives. Again, the choice of subunit strategy or objectives should reflect competitive contingencies and environmental uncertainties. The choice of unit form should be consistent with objectives/strategies. For example, in Torrence's laboratory, if his strategy is one of technological excellence, a discipline-based lab might be most appropriate. If, however, his objectives/strategy is dominated by product development, then he should adopt a product- or market-oriented laboratory.

At the organization level of analysis, the choice of organization form should reflect key competitive contingencies. Corporate strategic grouping sets the basic building blocks of the organization. Subunit managers must, in turn, make strategic grouping decisions for their subunits. These business unit, or functional area strategic, decisions must also be made based on dominant competitive issues and subunit objectives. Thus, the structure of an organization is likely to be made up of many different organization forms, each corresponding to local strategic requirements.

While the number of basic grouping options is limited, many combinations of forms can exist in one organization. For example, the top level of an organization might be organized by user/client, the next level

FIGURE 5-10    Combinations of Organization Forms: Grouping by Level

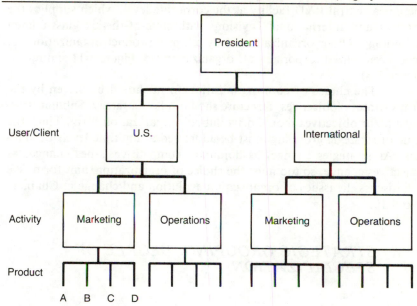

by activity, and the third level by output (see Figure 5-10). The grouping decisions made at the top of the organization are most critical because they constrain the configuration of the rest of the organization. The complexity in organization form will hinge on the complexity of the organization's strategy and its competitive environment. The greater the strategic and competitive complexity, the more complex the organization must be to handle the different strategic contingencies.

## Mixed organization forms

Organization form should be driven by strategy. Any one level of an organization should be focused on activity, outputs, or user/clients. It may be, however, that the organization has a particular focus (e.g., product or function) but has a common technology, a common customer base, a common manufacturing competence and/or a common staff organization. For example, at Corning Glass Works, glass-related technology is a common thread across the whole corporation. At 3M, bonding technology is the foundation on which almost all of its products are built.

If important commonalities exist across the organization, the organization should dedicate resources to this technology, market, or staff area, and adopt a mixed organization form. For example, at Corning, there is a central R&D facility at the corporate level, which supplies the Product and International Divisions with state-of-the-art glass-related technology. Other organizations may adopt a product organization yet have a centralized corporate staff organization (see Figure 5-11 and review Figure 5-8).

The choice of core organization form should be driven by the firm's strategy/objectives. Structure should follow strategy. Subunit strategy and/or objectives should drive subunit organization form. Thus, the issue of strategic grouping must be addressed at multiple levels of analysis. As strategies change, as dominant competitive issues change, as objectives change, so too must the choice of organization/unit form. We will discuss the issues of organization evolution and change in Chapters 9 and 10.

## STRATEGIC GROUPING: DEGREE OF SPECIALIZATION

The choice of organization form is the initial decision in organization design. The choices of form, at multiple levels of analysis, specify the basic units of the organization and its subunits. Once those choices are

FIGURE 5-11    Mixed Forms at One Level

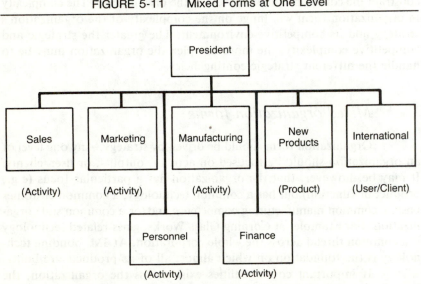

made, managers must also choose the degree of specialization for their subunits/organizations. For example, John Torrence could choose to have Research split from Advanced Development among the other disciplinary areas, or he could combine these two units into a larger, more general Development subunit. Similarly, a divisional general manager, after deciding on a functional structure for his or her division, must also make choices as to the degree of specialization in the division. For example, should the manager split Marketing from Sales or should the division invest in its own Development group?

Torrence's decision in his laboratory and the division general manager's decisions are both examples of choosing the degree of organizational specialization. Once management has chosen a form for the organization, they must then choose the set of subunits that will make up the organization. The degree of specialization can range from very highly specialized (that is, a number of specialized subunits each reporting to the manager) to a low degree of specialization (that is, a few subunits reporting to the manager) (see Figure 5-12).

## Managing the degree of specialization

When organizational form hinges on strategic considerations, the degree of specialization hinges on *work-related uncertainty*. Organizations must specialize enough to match task and/or environmental complexity. If task environments pose very different requirements, the subunit must develop a level of specialization to match environmental demands. For example, at AT&T, because of the enormous industry differences that emerged during the 1970s, many of the operating companies established industry groups reporting to the business manager's office. Similarly, if there is substantial task heterogeneity, the organization must specialize to match this source of uncertainty. If different tasks and/or task environments require specialized competence, the organization must be specialized to attend to those information-processing requirements.

If, however, there is relatively little environmental and/or task heterogeneity, then there need not be substantial specialization. For example, at Medtek, if the work in Research was not significantly different from that in Advanced Development, these groups could be combined. Similarly, if the market faced by the divisional general manager previously discussed is not rapidly changing, then Marketing need not be split from Sales. These two functions can be combined under one manager.

The degree of organizational specialization must be consistent with task and environmental demands. Complex and/or heterogeneous environmental demands require substantial organizational specialization. Those more focused units can attend to and deal with unique information-

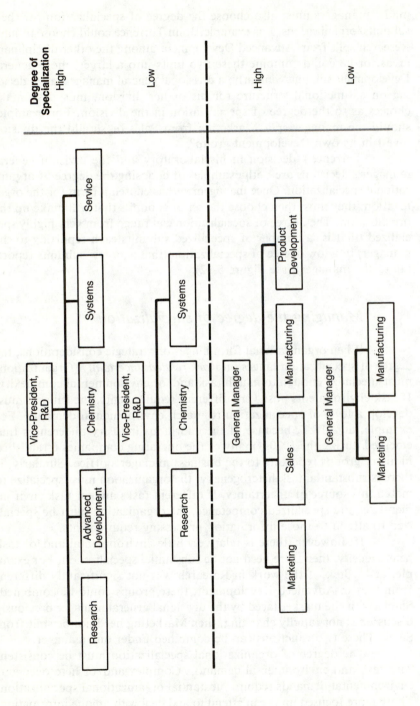

processing requirements. The increased costs of specialization are in service of the organization's increased ability to deal with uncertainty. On the other hand, simple environments and/or tasks require relatively less organizational specialization. If there is a mismatch between the degree of specialization (information-processing capacity) and work-related uncertainty, the organization will underperform. An organization can be overspecialized (that is, little uncertainty yet substantial specialization) as well as underspecialized (substantial uncertainty yet little specialization); both mismatches will be associated with lower organizational performance.

As with organizational form, the degree of organization specialization must be evaluated at each level of analysis. Thus in Figure 5-10, managers at each level of analysis must specify the degree of specialization. Following information-processing logic, the more complex and/or heterogeneous the organization's task environment, the more specialized the organization must be to deal with work-related uncertainty.

## ORGANIZATION POLITICS, INDIVIDUAL CAREERS, AND STRATEGIC GROUPING

Quite apart from settings where work is accomplished, organizations are also inherently political systems. Organizations are settings in which various groups have different degrees of power and in which decisions are outcomes of compromise and accommodation among coalitions of different interests. Because strategic grouping choices affect the allocation of scarce resources and shape the direction of organizations, the choice of organization form and degree of specialization will always trigger a response from the informal organization.

For example, at Medtek, any move to a project or matrix structure will be perceived as a threat to the disciplinary dominance of the laboratory. This perceived threat and loss of status is frequently associated with passive or aggressive resistance to change. Organizational politics, then, constrain the clear linkage between strategy and work requirements and strategic grouping choices. The choice of organization form and degree of specialization must take into account strategy and task requirements as well as political and social constraints.

Organizations are also settings in which individuals compete for positions and individual careers evolve. Choices of organization form and degree of specialization provide highly visible positions for managers to display their respective competencies. The choice of organization form and/or degree of specialization might also be shaped by the existence of several executives competing for limited senior positions. For example, at

Citibank prior to Walter Wriston's retirement as CEO in the mid-1980s, the issue of executive succession may have been part of the reason to establish three senior executive vice-presidents. The three competitors for Wriston's position each had distinct pieces of the bank. In this fashion, strategic grouping was used to accomplish the bank's strategy of decentralization and to provide data on the relative strengths and weaknesses of John Reed, Thomas Theobalt, and Hans Argumeller.

The choices of organization form and degree of specialization are, then, constrained and shaped by political factors and individual career concerns within the organization. The choice of organization form and degree of specialization must take into account strategic and task requirements shaped by the organization's political system and the existence of senior managers to effectively staff positions that are associated with different organization forms (see Figure 5-13). Chapters 8 and 10 both discuss the impact of career and political factors in the strategic design process and in the management of change.

## SUMMARY

**Opening case revisited:**

John Torrence could not make decisions about his laboratory's structure without greater strategic direction. Torrence and his senior managers developed a business/technology strategy, which centered on being a technology leader (i.e., a me-first producer of proprietary new products). Given their commitment to superior technology, Medtek's management rejected market-, project-, and/or customer-based forms for the laboratory in favor of a disciplinary form. Further, because Torrence's team felt there were substantial task and time-frame differences between Research and Advanced Development, these two areas were not combined into a single Research Department. Given these strategic grouping decisions, Torrence's team still had to make a range of decisions focusing on structural linking and management control systems (see Chapter 6).

Strategic grouping is the first and most important design step. Strategic grouping involves choosing the appropriate organization form at multiple levels of analysis and specifying the degree of specialization for each level. The choice of organization form must be driven by key strategic contingencies. Alternative choices must be weighed against strategy/

FIGURE 5-13    Strategic Grouping

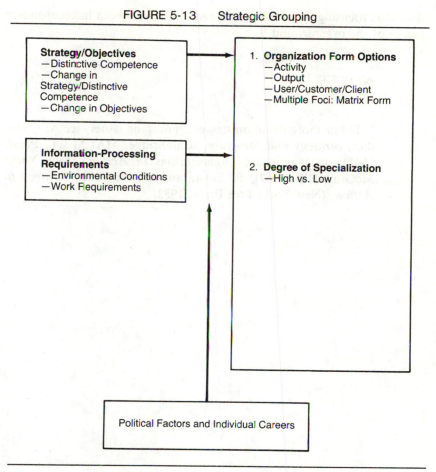

**Strategy/Objectives**
—Distinctive Competence
—Change in Strategy/Distinctive Competence
—Change in Objectives

1. **Organization Form Options**
—Activity
—Output
—User/Customer/Client
—Multiple Foci: Matrix Form

**Information-Processing Requirements**
—Environmental Conditions
—Work Requirements

2. **Degree of Specialization**
—High vs. Low

Political Factors and Individual Careers

objective requirements. The degree of specialization is driven by information-processing requirements; the greater the task/environmental complexity, the greater the degree of required specialization. As choices of organization form and degree of specialization affect the distribution of power and control and affect the careers of senior managers, these choices will always affect an organization's political equilibrium. Organizational politics and individual careers, then, moderate the linkage between strategy and work requirements and strategic grouping choices.

Strategic grouping is not just an issue for senior management. It is the first issue for any manager interested in designing a business unit. These decisions define the organization's architecture as well as a set of positions in the management hierarchy (review Figures 5-1 through 5-10). Strategic grouping decisions set the stage for strategic linking, a series of decisions focusing on coordination and control between interdependent pieces of the organization.

## NOTES

1. For more detail on strategic grouping issues, see A. Chandler, *Strategy and Structure*, (Cambridge, MA: M.I.T. Press, 1962); J. Thompson, *Organizations in Action*, (New York: McGraw-Hill, 1967); B. Yavitz and W. Newman, *Strategy in Action*, (New York: Free Press, 1982).

# 6

# Strategic Linking: Designing Formal Coordination Mechanisms

**Cases:**

Jean Shaeffer, President of Federal Engineering, is grappling with an important decision for her engineering products firm (see Figure 6-1). Currently the industry leader in scientific instruments and process control products, her firm has not gotten any of the burgeoning systems business. This new market requires the production of integrated systems tailored to different user-needs. While Federal Engineering, with its divisional structure, has been able to provide first quality instruments, it has not been able to produce competitive systems. Somehow, Federal's systems have been late and of low quality and have generated substantial customer dissatisfaction. Shaeffer's hunch is that while her firm has excellent technical talent, the distinct groups just do not work well together. There are priority difficulties, a lack of information sharing, and a lack of working together for the good of the systems business. Shaeffer's dilemma is that she must not jeopardize the instrument business while attacking the firm's problems in the systems area.

Roger Laffer, Senior Strategy Officer for Office Products Corporation, has been asked by the firm's CEO to help come up with an institutional framework for corporate technology transfer (see Figure 6-2). While this firm has been widely known for its technological and market excellence in computers, printers, and office products, the firm has a dismal record in capitalizing on technologies across existing business units. Laffer feels that the corpo-

FIGURE 6-1    Federal Engineering

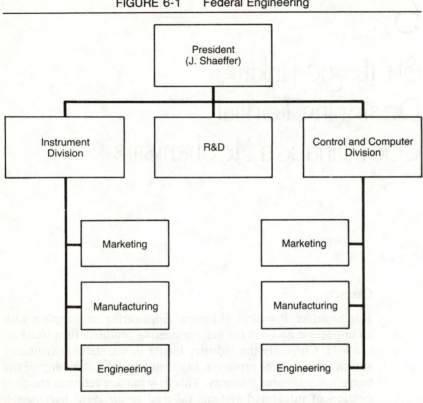

ration's focus on distinct products/market niches hinders its ability to deal with opportunities that did not neatly fit into corporate categories. Laffer wonders whether a revised structure, along with top management support, could provide an institutional infrastructure to support technology transfer.

Both Shaeffer and Laffer are dealing with problems of strategic linking. Both must develop a set of formal linking mechanisms that will work to enhance, encourage, and facilitate coordination between distinct groups in their firms. Strategic linking issues follow directly from strategic grouping choices. Strategic grouping focuses resources by product, market, discipline, or geography. This grouping of resources puts some resources together *and* splits other resources. For example, a disciplinary-organized pharmaceutical laboratory focuses attention on disciplines but scatters individuals who are interested in therapeutic areas. In a product organization, functional expertise is split among product areas. Strategic

FIGURE 6-2     Office Products Company

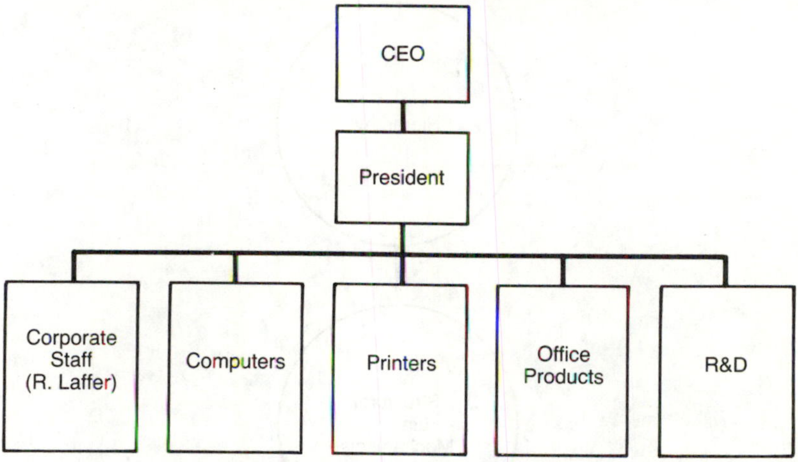

linking involves choosing formal structures that link units that have been split during strategic grouping. Once strategic grouping decisions have been made, the next step is to coordinate, or link, the units so that the firm can operate as an integrated whole.

Where grouping decisions are driven by strategy considerations, strategic linking is driven by the degree of **task interdependence** between areas. Different degrees of task interdependence require different types of formal linking mechanisms. The objective is to build linking mechanisms that allow adequate information processing between groups. Linking mechanisms that are not adequate to handle necessary information will result in poorly coordinated work. Those linking mechanisms that are more extensive than necessary will hinder information flow and result in unnecessary cost. This chapter discusses different types of work interdependence, presents a range of formal linking mechanisms, and concludes with a methodology for making linking decisions. We leave for Chapter 8 the issue of using the informal organization to achieve coordination across areas (see Figure 6-3).

# VARIETIES OF TASK INTERDEPENDENCE

Strategic grouping results in a set of groups that are dedicated to product, markets, function, and/or discipline. Strategic grouping provides the basic architecture of the firm at each level of analysis (see Chapter 5).

FIGURE 6-3     A Range of Formal Linking Mechanisms

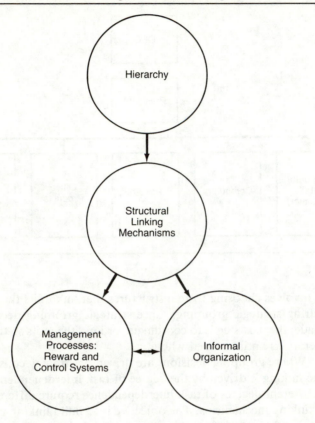

Strategic linking involves choosing those sets of formal linking mechanisms to coordinate the different groups so the organization functions as a whole. For example, at Federal Engineering, Jean Shaeffer must choose a set of formal linking mechanisms to link the two divisions together in service of the systems business. Similarly, at Medtek (see Chapter 5), John Torrence must choose a set of formal linking mechanisms to link the different disciplinary areas in service of product development.

Linking follows directly from grouping and, as with strategic grouping, must be accomplished at multiple levels of analysis. Our design problem involves choosing the right set of linking mechanisms to deal with: (1) work flows between distinct units, (2) the need for disciplinary- or staff-based professionals to have contact across the firm, and (3) work flows associated with emergencies, crises, or other nonroutine events.

The conceptual thread across work flow, disciplinary linkages, and work flows under crisis conditions is work-related interdependence. Managers choose linking mechanisms to deal with this source of uncertainty. The greater the task interdependence, the greater the need for coordination and joint problem solving. The more complex the degree of work/task interdependence, the more complex the formal linkage devices must be to handle work-related uncertainty. On the other hand, groups that are only weakly interdependent have relatively little need for coordination and joint problem solving and therefore need simple formal linking devices.

Consider branch banks located throughout a city. Each branch bank runs essentially independently of each other except for the common sharing of advertising and marketing resources. Similarly, business units within a diversified firm with completely different product/market niches are also essentially independent of each other except for those corporate resources that are shared between divisions (e.g., technology, staff). Both of these examples illustrate **pooled interdependence**. Units that operate independently but are part of the same organization and therefore share scarce resources must deal with the pooled nature of their interdependence. Units with pooled interdependence have a minimal amount of coordination and linking requirements (see Figure 6-4).

At Olympic Oil, the Petroleum Products Division extracts petroleum from the ground and provides the raw material for the Polymer Chemistry Division (see Figure 6-5). This division makes a variety of products that various end-use divisions use in the production of consumer and construction products. Similarly, in the back office of a bank, checks move through a series of groups before they exit the bank. These examples illustrate **sequential interdependence** (review Figure 6-4). Sequentially interdependent units must deal with a greater degree and variety of problem-solving and coordination requirements than units that have pooled interdependence. Groups that have sequential interdependence must attend to close coordination and timing so that work flows remain smooth and uninterrupted; each unit in the work flow is dependent on prior units.

At Medtek, Marketing must work with R&D and with Production in the development of new products. Each functional area must be in close contact with the others to ensure the synthesis of market, technological, and production considerations. Similarly, in an advertising agency, the media, creative, and account services areas must work closely with each other in the development of ad campaigns for their clients. These examples illustrate **reciprocal interdependence**, that is, interdependence in which each group must work with each other unit in the production of a common product (review Figure 6-4). Reciprocal interdependence

FIGURE 6-4      Forms of Interdependence

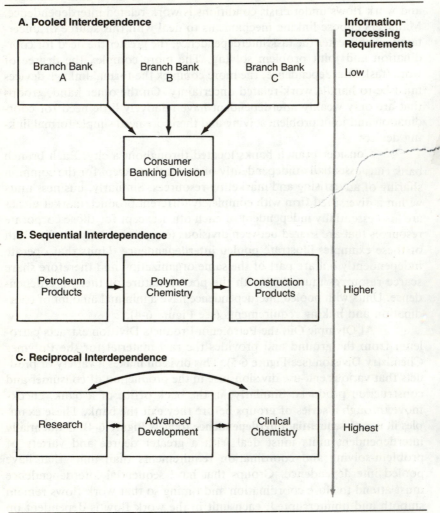

**A. Pooled Interdependence**

**Information-Processing Requirements**

Branch Bank A → Branch Bank B → Branch Bank C

Consumer Banking Division

Low

**B. Sequential Interdependence**

Petroleum Products → Polymer Chemistry → Construction Products

Higher

**C. Reciprocal Interdependence**

Research ↔ Advanced Development ↔ Clinical Chemistry

Highest

imposes substantial coordination and problem-solving requirements between units; no one unit can accomplish its task without the active contribution of each other unit.

Pooled, sequential, and reciprocal interdependence represent different degrees of work-related interdependence. Reciprocal interdependence imposes greater coordination costs and complexity than sequential, which, in turn, requires greater coordination than pooled interdependence.

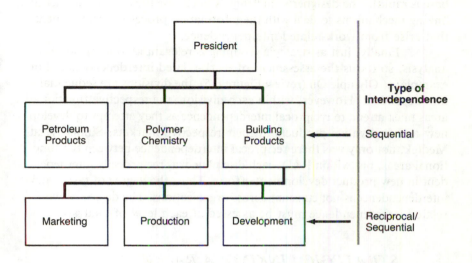

Beyond work flows, accentuated task interdependence can also arise in emergency, temporary, or crisis situations, in which units that normally only pool their activities must suddenly work together. For example, in our branch bank example, if one part of town suffers a black out, then the other branch banks must work together more closely to deal with the emergency. Similarly, independent product divisions that share a common technology must work together for those unique corporate ventures that attempt to combine the strengths of the two divisions.

Finally, quite apart from work flow considerations, knowledge-based staff and/or professionals must retain contact across organization boundaries or they will become overly specialized and/or lose touch with the state-of-the-art in their respective fields. The greater the rate of change in the discipline or staff areas, the greater the professionally anchored interdependence. At Warner-Lambert, for example, biologists in various areas of the corporation held monthly seminars to inform each other of current biological developments. This need for continual updating was much less critical in the more routine toxicological areas.

Whether driven by work flows, crises, or professionally anchored need for collaboration, these differing degrees of work-related interdependence impose different information processing requirements. Those units that have pooled interdependence (or in which the rate of change of the underlying knowledge base is low) have fewer coordination demands and information processing requirements than units that have reciprocal interdependence (or in which the rate of change of the underlying knowledge base is rapid). The designer's challenge is to choose the appropriate set of linking mechanisms to deal with the information-processing requirements that arise from work-related interdependence.

Finally, just as strategic grouping is relevant at multiple levels of analysis, so too is the assessment of work-related interdependence. For example, at Olympic Oil (review Figure 6-5), the divisions are sequentially interdependent. However, within each division, the respective functional areas must attend to reciprocal interdependence as they attempt to develop new and innovative products in their respective markets. Similarly, at Medtek, not only was there reciprocal interdependence between the functional areas, but within R&D, each discipline was reciprocally interdependent in new product development efforts. Thus, the degree of task/work interdependence is not constant across organizations. The degree of work-related interdependence must be assessed at each level of analysis.

## STRATEGIC LINKING: A RANGE OF LINKING MECHANISMS

Various types of formal mechanisms can be used to link, or coordinate, the efforts of organizational groups. Our objective is to choose those structural linking mechanisms that provide adequate information flows, procedures, and structures to deal with the information requirements imposed by work-related interdependence. Informal mechanisms to achieve coordination between units will be discussed in Chapter 8. Formal linking mechanisms that are not sufficient to handle linking requirements will result in poorly coordinated work. Those linking mechanisms that are more extensive than need be will result in unnecessary costs and overcomplexity. Structural linking mechanisms can be analyzed in terms of their ability to handle information flows and complex problem-solving requirements.[1]

### Hierarchy

The most simple form of structural linking is the **hierarchy:** the formal distribution of power and authority. The hierarchy of authority follows directly from grouping decisions. For example, in a divisional structure, the divisional general managers report to the president of the firm, while functional managers report to their respective divisional general managers (review Figure 6-1). Coordination and linking between managers at the same level can be accomplished via their common boss. The common boss serves as an information channel, can exercise control over how much and what types of information move between groups, and can adjudicate problems that arise in his or her area.

The formal hierarchy is the simplest and one of the most pervasive formal linking mechanisms. Focused, sustained, and consistent behavior by the manager can both direct and set the stage for the effective coordination between organizational groups. The hierarchy is, however, a limited linking mechanism. Because of inherent cognitive/information-processing capacity, even modest amounts of task interdependence, exceptions, crises, or environmental uncertainty can overload the individual manager. When linking requirements begin to overload the first common supervisor (e.g., see earlier Shaeffer, Laffer examples), other formal mechanisms must be used to complement the manager as a linking mechanism.

## Structural linking

*Liaison roles* • At Federal Engineering, the development of process control systems requires the close coordination between the Instrument and Control Divisions. While some linking occurs via the hierarchy (i.e., through Shaeffer), much more intense problem solving occurs between two **liaison individuals**. John O'Connor and Phil Dinsky, respected members of the two divisions, are the point-men on the systems business. These two individuals serve as sources of information and expertise for problems and as contacts and advisors on systems work that affects their two divisions.

O'Connor and Dinsky represent formal liaison roles—formal roles that serve as information conduits and initiators of problem-solving endeavors deep in the organization. These liaison roles are responsible for enhanced information flows and coordination between units, although they rarely have authority to back up their positions. The liaison role is not usually a full-time responsibility but rather is done in conjunction with other activities (see Figure 6-6).

*Cross-unit groups* • At Federal Engineering, the Air Force is a particularly important customer; Federal Engineering supplies the Air Force with a range of products and services. There are numerous Air Force complaints, however, of sloppy coordination and incomplete and/or inconsistent information among Federal Engineering professionals. To provide focused Air Force coordination between the different divisions, Shaeffer convened an Air Force integrating committee. This committee brought all key Federal Engineering actors together—a cross-unit group—to ensure a common posture toward the Air Force (see Figure 6-7).

The Air Force coordinating committee is one example of a range of possible group-based formal coordinating mechanisms. Groups made up of task-relevant representatives meet to focus on particular clients,

FIGURE 6-6     Liaison Roles

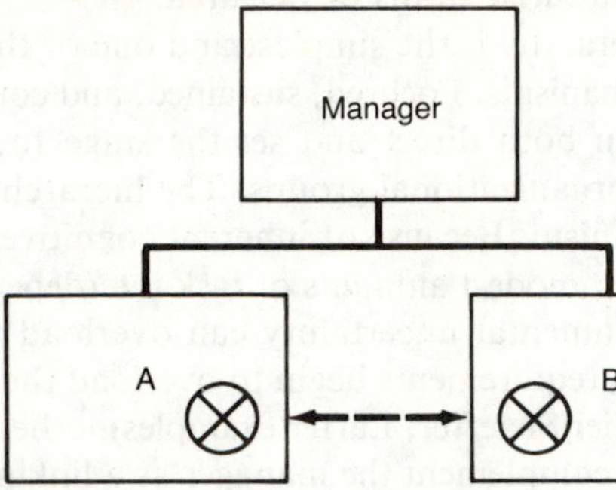

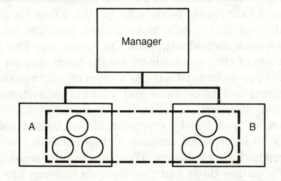

FIGURE 6-7     Cross-Unit Groups

products, markets, and/or problems. These groups can be permanent, temporary, or ad hoc. Their objective is to assure that relevant expertise comes together to deal with their joint task/problem.

In contrast with liaison roles, cross-unit groups provide a more extensive forum for information exchange, for coordination, and for the resolution of conflict between work units. Although these task forces, teams, or groups may form as need be, it may also be appropriate to design cross-unit groups into the structure if there are ongoing cross-unit projects. In a medical center, for example, a representative group of individuals from the key divisions might be responsible for establishing and adjusting guidelines and processes that affect work flows across divisions.

*Integrator role or department* • If problem-solving requirements increase and more decisions affecting multiple groups must be made at lower levels of the organization, teams and/or liaison individuals might not be sufficient. Cross-unit groups may result in no one person feeling accountable for the total performance of the group. Conflicts sometimes arise within cross-unit groups or between liaison individuals, yet the first common boss might not have the expertise and/or time to adjudicate these differences. A solution to the need for real-time problem solving and for bringing general management's point of view to lower levels in the organization is to appoint an individual as **integrator**. This integrator role is responsible for taking a general management point of view in helping multiple-work groups accomplish a joint task, such as a specific product or project (see Figure 6-8).

Product, brand, geographic, and account managers are examples of formal roles created to bring a general management perspective to specialized managers who bring focused expertise, yet relatively narrow concerns to team meetings. Integrators have the formal responsibility of achieving coordination across the organization. While integrators report to senior management, they usually do not have formal authority to direct their functional and/or disciplinary colleagues. Because of this dotted-line relationship to members of their team, integrators must rely on expertise, interpersonal competence, and team and conflict-resolution skills to shape the efforts of frequently recalcitrant team members.

Integrator roles must acquire functional or disciplinary resources to accomplish their work. When there are several projects, accounts, or products, each of these must compete with one another for resources. For example, in a functional organization, if there are five new product

FIGURE 6-8    Integrators (Project, Brand, Program, Account Managers)

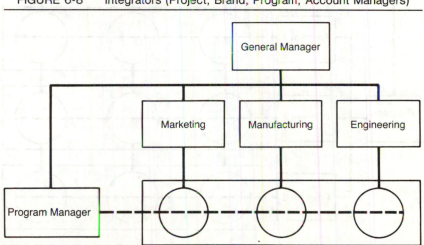

efforts, each of these must acquire scarce resources and attention from functional managers. To increase the power of the product/project organization and to help coordinate resources among products, a product development department is sometimes created (see Figure 6-9).

In product/project organizations, the product side of the organization has its own senior manager who reports along the same line as the functional managers. This senior manager formally represents the product side of the organization at senior levels and assists in resource allocation across projects. However, the functional organization still reports to its functional supervisors and has a dotted-line relationship with the project/product manager. While our example has centered on project/product integrator roles, the role is quite general. It is a role to counter the consequences of strategic grouping, to achieve coordination and real-time problem solving at lower levels of complex organizations.

FIGURE 6-9     Integrating Department

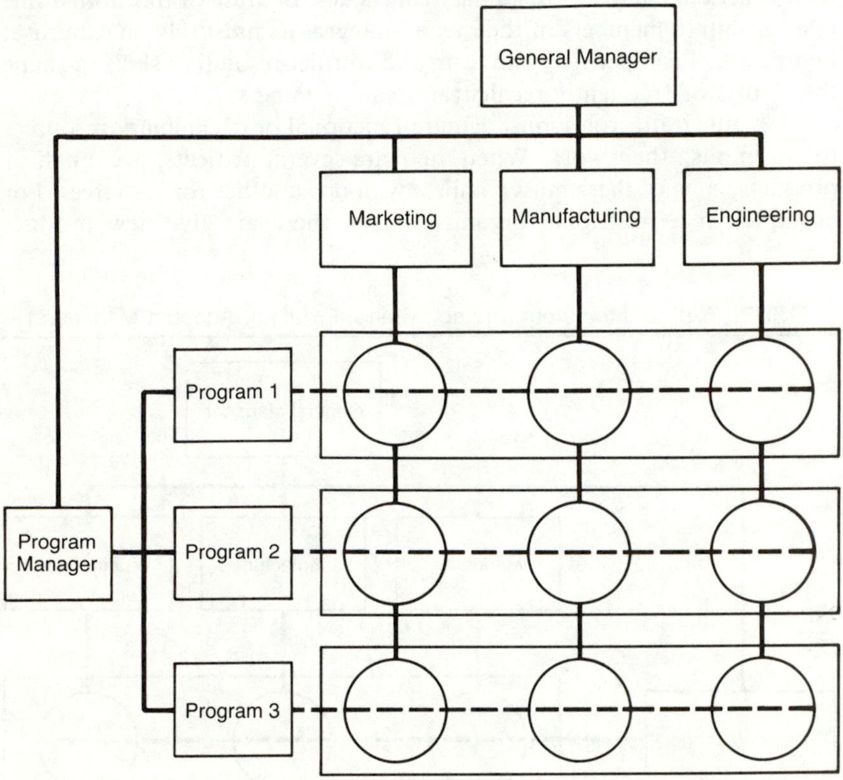

*Matrix structures* • Some strategies require equal attention to several strategic contingencies, for example, products and markets or product and geography. Similarly, in highly uncertain environments with highly interdependent tasks, great pressures for coordination may come from both the functional and product sides of the organization. Whenever strategy requires the simultaneous maximization of several dimensions (e.g., product, market, geographic, time) and/or when information-processing requirements demand simultaneous consideration of several dimensions, integrating roles are not sufficient to handle the enormous information-processing requirements. When it is important to give equal attention to several critical contingencies and when information-processing demands are substantial, **matrix structures** are appropriate.

A matrix organization structurally improves coordination between multiple perspectives by balancing the power between dimensions of the organization and by installing systems and roles to achieve multiple objectives at once. For example, an R&D facility that wants to maximize disciplinary competence *and* product focus might invest in a matrix structure. Directors of the different laboratories would then report to both their disciplinary and product managers. The dotted-line relationship (seen in the integrator role) becomes solid; key members of the laboratory have two bosses.

Figure 6-10 presents a matrix organization structure. It has two chains of command. On the right side, the functional departments continue to exist. The organization still benefits from the information exchange and control provided by the grouping of people by function. On the left is another chain of command, with a product manager for each major new product coordinating the activities of individuals across functional groups. Thus, those managers within each function who head product activities report to two bosses at once, a functional boss and a product boss. In this way, information is processed both within and across functional groups and coordination of different product-oriented activities is achieved.

Matrix structures are very complex. They require dual systems, roles, controls, and rewards. Systems, structures, and processes must be developed to handle both dimensions of the matrix. Further, matrix managers must deal with the difficulties of sharing a common subordinate, while the common subordinate must face off against two bosses. As seen in Figure 6-11, the general manager is the single boss, where each of the sides of the matrix come together. This individual must assure equal power and influence to each side of the matrix. Otherwise the organization will revert back to a single-focus organization. Below the matrix manager there is also a clear hierarchy. His or her subordinates report to one boss. The matrix is most directly felt by the matrix manager and the two matrix

FIGURE 6-10     Matrix Organization

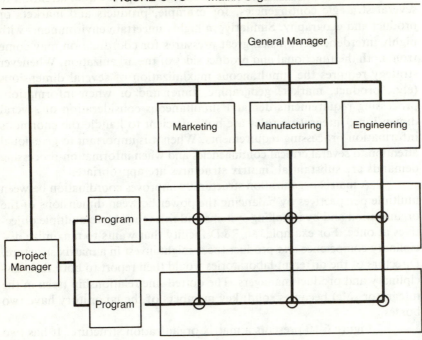

supervisors. It is this relatively narrow slice of the organization that really sees matrix systems, roles, procedures, and processes. This set of four roles must constantly balance the pressures and conflicts in a structure that attempts to work several strategic directions at once.

While the matrix structure is the most complex and conflictual linking mechanism, it is also the only structure that attempts to maximize several strategically important considerations at once. Given its complexity and inherent instability, a matrix structure should be reserved for situations in which no other linking alternative is workable.[2]

## Making structural linking decisions

*Costs and benefits of linking options* • Structural linking mechanisms vary by cost and resources utilized, their dependence on the informal organization, and their inherent information-processing capacities. The essence of making linking decisions is to choose those formal linking mechanisms that most effectively handle work-related interdepen-

FIGURE 6-11    Matrix Organization: Another Perspective

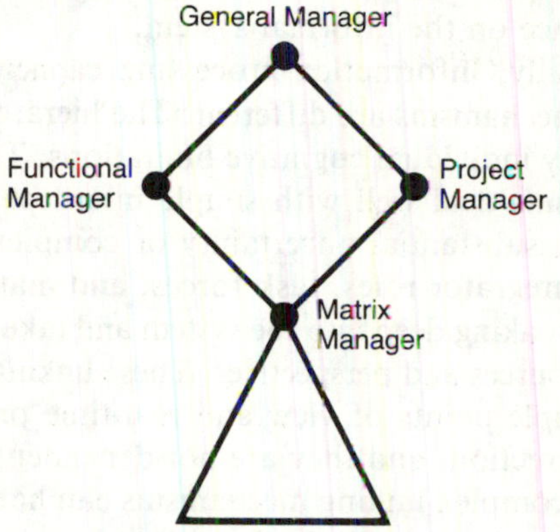

dence. Using overly complex linking mechanisms will be too costly and inefficient, while using too simple linking mechanisms will not get the work done. The hierarchy of structural linking mechanisms can be evaluated along the following set of dimensions:

1. The cost and/or amount of resources devoted to each mechanism differs greatly. The formal hierarchy or liaison roles require sustained attention to coordination by a few key individuals. Matrix structures, on the other hand, require dual structures, systems, and procedures. Matrix structures also require time, energy, and effort devoted to committees and teams that attend to both axes of the matrix. The more extensive the linking mechanism in terms of individuals involved, systems, and procedures, the more resources must be devoted and the more costly the linking mechanism.

2. Formal linking mechanisms also differ in their dependence on the informal organization. Where the hierarchy and some liaison roles rest firmly on the formal organization, cross-group units, integrator roles, and matrix structures depend more and more on a healthy informal organization. Those more complex linking mechanisms actually build on organization conflict. These linking mechanisms require an informal organization that can handle the ambiguity and conflict associated with substantial work-related interdependence. Indeed, without an informal organization that deals openly with conflict, that has collaborative norms and values, and that can deal with the complexities of

dual-boss relations, matrix organizations will not work. Thus, the more complex the formal linking mechanism, the greater the dependence on the informal system.

3. Finally, information-processing capacities of the various linking mechanisms are different. The hierarchy and liaisons are limited by individual cognitive limitations. These simple linking mechanisms deal well with simple interdependence but cannot deal with substantial uncertainty or complex work interdependence. Integrator roles, task forces, and matrix structures push decision making deep into the system and take advantage of many more resources and perspectives. These linking mechanisms allow for multiple points of view and real-time problem solving and error correction, and they are not dependent on individuals.

More complex linking mechanisms can handle more information and deal more effectively with uncertainty than can simpler linking mechanisms. Liaison roles can only relay limited amounts of information and, while they can identify issues needing coordination, their ability to resolve conflicts is limited. Cross-unit groups can identify issues needing coordination and can involve the requisite number of individuals in inter-unit problem solving. Figure 6-12 compares information-processing capacity with cost and dependence on the informal organization for the set of structural linking devices.

*Making strategic linking decisions* • Jean Shaeffer at Federal Engineering required a structure that would continue to produce top-quality scientific instruments *and* would compete more effectively for the systems business. Shaeffer decided to keep her product organization but to add a systems-business manager. Reflecting the importance of the systems business, this systems manager reported directly to Shaeffer and was

FIGURE 6-12    Consequences of Structural Linking Mechanisms

|  | Cost | Dependence on Informal Organization | Information-Processing Capacity |
|---|---|---|---|
|  | Low | Low | Low |
| Hierarchy | ↑ | ↑ | ↑ |
| Liaison | | | |
| Cross-Unit Groups | | | |
| Integrator Roles/Departments | | | |
| Matrix Organization | ↓ | ↓ | ↓ |
|  | High | High | High |

fully responsible for the systems business. The systems manager was evaluated on systems business and acquired resources from relevant divisions within Federal Engineering. Divisional employees working on systems business were evaluated by their divisional managers as well as the systems manager.

Roger Laffer did some diagnostic work on his firm's technology transfer problem and discovered that there was no corporate vehicle to capitalize on technology transfer opportunities. While the divisions had plenty of ideas, there was no corporate instrument to evaluate and/or take action on those ideas. Laffer recommended the creation of a technology transfer board. This committee would be made up of senior technologists and divisional general managers and would be a corporate focal point for technology transfer. The committee was charged with evaluating, pushing, and funding technology transfer opportunities throughout the corporation. This technology transfer board was headed by a senior manager with both technological and market competence and was actively supported by the president and CEO.

Shaeffer and Laffer both faced problems in strategic linking. Shaeffer's organization had to deal with substantial work-related interdependence and considerable time pressure. Shaeffer's choice of a project organization with a powerful project manager reflects the demands of the reciprocal interdependence between divisions. Laffer's task force/committee solution to his firm's technology transfer problem reflects the pooled nature of the work interdependence and the weak-to-moderate perceived time pressure. Consistent with work requirements, Shaeffer chose a complex set of linking mechanisms, whereas Laffer chose a simpler, committee-based linking mechanism.

More generally, the problem in strategic linking is to choose those *sets* of formal linking mechanisms that effectively deal with work-related interdependence. The linking mechanisms discussed here are not mutually exclusive. Rather, managers must choose those sets of linking devices that are able to deal with the work-related uncertainty. For example, at Federal Engineering, Shaeffer must utilize the hierarchy, liaison individuals, cross-group teams, and project organization, all in service of the systems effort. Shaeffer added the project organization only because simpler linking mechanisms were not sufficient for the systems business. Thus, more complex formal linking mechanisms are utilized to deal with work interdependence with which more simple mechanisms are unable to cope.

Structural linking involves choosing the set of formal linking mechanisms that deals with work-related interdependence. Managers must balance the cost of more complex linking mechanisms with their increased information-processing capacity. Structural linking mechanisms must be extensive enough to handle information-processing requirements. Overly complex linking mechanisms will be costly to the organization in terms of time, money, energy, and effort. For example, a matrix organization to handle Laffer's problem would only create confusion and chaos in his technology transfer efforts. On the other hand, linking mechanisms that are not adequate to meet work, professional, or problem demands will result in poorly coordinated work. For example, if Shaeffer used a committee or task force to deal with the systems business, it is highly unlikely that the systems business would be taken seriously throughout Federal Engineering.

The choice of structural linking mechanisms should, then, be based on work-related interdependence. Those more complex linking requirements require more complex formal linking devices. Managers must choose those sets of linking mechanisms that match the information-processing demands of their unit's work interdependence. A mismatch between information-processing requirements and the choice of linking devices will be associated with relatively poor coordination and lower organization performance (see Figure 6-13).

## STRATEGIC LINKING IN ACTION

Formal linking mechanisms address the communication and information-processing needs that arise from grouping decisions. When grouping decisions both group together and split apart resources, linking mechanisms work to achieve coordination between interdependent units. As grouping decisions are made at several levels of analysis, so too are linking decisions. At Olympic Oil (review Figure 6-5), management must make linking decisions at the corporate, divisional, and functional levels. As each level deals with different degrees of work interdependence, the choices of structural linking mechanisms will differ. For example, the sequential interdependence at the corporate level can be handled via a senior team or committee; more complex linking mechanisms are required to deal with reciprocal interdependence within the division. Linking decisions, like grouping decisions, are important at each level of an organization.

Structural linking is an important managerial tool. Whereas strategic grouping decisions are single decisions made at each level of analysis, there may be a host of structural linking mechanisms within a particular unit. For example, at Medtek's R&D facility, structural linking might be accomplished via a matrix organization throughout the laboratory. Further, special task forces might be utilized to deal with the impact of new technologies on the organization, a top team might be convened to deal with a new competitive threat, and informal committees

FIGURE 6-13     Strategic Linking: Formal Coordinating Mechanisms

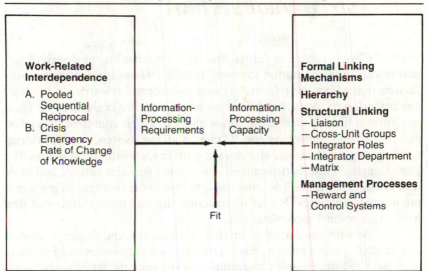

**Work-Related Interdependence**

A. Pooled
   Sequential
   Reciprocal
B. Crisis
   Emergency
   Rate of Change
   of Knowledge

Information-Processing Requirements

Information-Processing Capacity

Fit

**Formal Linking Mechanisms**

**Hierarchy**

**Structural Linking**
—Liaison
—Cross-Unit Groups
—Integrator Roles
—Integrator Department
—Matrix

**Management Processes**
—Reward and
  Control Systems

—Performance is a function of choosing that set of formal linking mechanisms to deal with work-related interdependence.

—As interdependence changes, so too should linking mechanisms change.

—Structural linking is required at multiple levels of analysis.

might be established to share expertise across disciplines within the laboratory. Linking, then, can be a powerful and flexible tool to deal with the different coordination requirements that exist within all organizations. Again, the choice of linking mechanism must be contingent on work-related interdependence.

Finally, as work interdependence shifts over time, so too should the choice of linking mechanisms. For example, if Laffer's technology transfer board (a simple linking mechanism) comes up with a viable candidate for internal development, the increased task interdependence between divisions will require some form of project organization to provide direction and real-time coordination efforts. Again, the choice of linking mechanisms must deal with the requisite task interdependence. As task interdependencies are not fixed, neither can our choices of structural linking mechanisms be fixed (review Figure 6-13).

## MANAGEMENT PROCESSES: REWARD AND CONTROL SYSTEMS

Closely related to formal linking mechanisms is the design of formal reward and evaluation systems. Individuals are motivated by those factors that affect their formal as well as informal rewards. Individuals pay attention to those dimensions on which they are evaluated. As such, any formal linking mechanism must also be tied to complementary formal reward and control systems. If there is an inconsistency between structural linking mechanisms and reward patterns, coordination will suffer. For example, if a sales department is rewarded for sales volume and manufacturing is rewarded for gross margin, then these two groups are working at cross-purposes. No set of structural linking mechanisms can deal with these reward inconsistencies.

As with the choice of linking mechanisms, the choice of reward and control systems must be contingent on work requirements. More complex tasks require complex and subtle reward systems, while simple tasks require elementary reward systems. For example, at Federal Engineering, members of the systems team must be evaluated both for quality instruments as well as for their contribution to the systems business. These more complex reward systems must assess hard and soft criteria, both of which are critical for successful systems products.

Whatever the nature of the reward and/or control systems, they should (1) have clearly specified and operational objectives, (2) reward the total task as well as component tasks, (3) eliminate zero-sum situations, and (4) clearly link performance to valued outcomes. Bonus and incentive systems should be clearly linked to subunit performance and organizational performance. At both Federal Engineering and Laffer's office products company, the choices of structural linking mechanisms must be bolstered with formal reward and incentive systems that clearly evaluate and reward individuals for their contributions to the systems business and technology transfer.[3]

## SUMMARY

### Medtek revisited:

At Medtek, John Torrence's disciplinary-focused laboratory had to simultaneously support existing products and develop fundamentally new clinical diagnostic products. Those mature products only required sequential coupling between disciplinary areas, where new product development involved substantial problem solving and coordination between each disciplinary area. To handle these diverse task requirements, Torrence initiated multiple formal linkage mechanisms. Project managers were appointed to see to it that new products received sustained attention across the laboratory. These project managers reported to Torrence and had the responsibility (but not the authority) to get new products out on time and on budget. Project controls and rewards were developed to enhance the project manager's influence. Incremental product improvements on the standard product line were coordinated via the hierarchy. Thus, the different task interdependence demands were managed with quite different formal linking mechanisms.

A vital aspect of organization design is the choice of formal devices to achieve coordination between work units. Linking mechanisms range from simple mechanisms, such as the formal hierarchy and liaison roles, to much more complex approaches, such as matrix structures. As work interdependence and uncertainty increase, more complex linking mechanisms are required. Managers must choose the set of linking mechanisms that fits the organization's linking requirements. Reward and control systems must also be designed to complement structural linking mechanisms. As linking requirements change, so too must the choice of formal linking mechanisms. Structural linking is only one vehicle for achieving coordination between units. Indeed, those more complex linking mechanisms depend on a healthy informal organization. Chapter 8 discusses the informal organization as a complementary way of achieving coordination.

## NOTES

1. Our linking ideas build on much earlier work, including J. Galbraith, *Designing Complex Organizations*, (Reading, MA: Addison-Wesley, 1973); L. Sayles and M. Chandler, *Managing Large Systems*, (New York: Harper & Row, 1971); L. Sayles, "Matrix Management: The Structure with a Future," *Organizational Dynamics* (Autumn 1976); R. Katz and T. Allen, "Project Performance and the Locus of Influence in the R&D Matrix,"

*Academy of Management Journal* 28 (1985) 67–87; A. Van de Ven, A. Delbecq, and R. Koenig, "Determinants of Coordination Modes Within Organizations," *American Sociological Review* 41 (1976) 322–37.

2. See S. Davis, and P. Lawrence, *Matrix*, (Reading, MA: Addison-Wesley, 1977) for an in-depth discussion of matrix organizations.

3. For much more detail on reward and control systems and their linkage to organization design, see E. Lawler, *Pay and Organization Development*, (Reading, MA: Addison-Wesley, 1981); R. Dunbar, "Designs for Organizational Control," in P. Nystrom and W. Starbuck, eds., *Handbook of Organization Design*, (New York: Oxford University Press, 1981); E. Lawler and J. Rhode, *Information and Control in Organizations*, (Santa Monica, CA: Goodyear, 1976).

# 7

# Applied Issues in Organization Design: Decentralization and the Design of Staff Groups

**Case:**

Ben Hayes, Chairman of the Board and CEO of General Industries Corporation, was reviewing notes he had made during recent sessions with managers in the company. As part of the normal management development programs, Ben met at the corporate training center with groups of middle managers going through various management training sessions. Ben typically met informally with a group on Friday afternoon for several hours to hear their views and answer their questions about the company.

Following each session, Ben took a few moments to jot down some notes about the issues the managers had raised. Ben was now looking at these notes and noticing that two issues seemed to come up over and over again. First, middle managers complained about "corporate" decision making. Their view was that any decision that had to go to the corporate headquarters would inevitably be slowed down, so much so that important business opportunities were being lost through inaction. Decisions also seemed to require a lot of paperwork to back up recommendations, even when they were routine and even trivial. People also saw a lack of clarity about who was empowered to make what decisions at what level of the organization, and about who else had to be involved in different decisions.

A second issue concerned complaints about the corporate staff. The people in line jobs saw the staff as too big, too powerful, and too contentious. The staff seemed to slow up major projects or decisions and, even worse, add to the work load by making frequent requests for information that required a lot of time and effort for responses. In the midst of cost pressures throughout the business, people were wondering what they were getting for all of the money being spent on the corporate staff. During one session, it even slipped out that the operating units referred to the large, new, impressive corporate headquarters building (where the staff units were located) as "the cave of the big wind."

General Industries is a diversified company with various operations and businesses in light manufacturing and middle-to-high technology industries. With more than 150,000 employees, it includes 23 major operating units, companies, or subsidiaries, many of which operate in both domestic and international markets. For a long time, General Industries operated as a holding company. The chairman and president, along with a very small staff, presided over a large number of operating units that had great autonomy and were measured basically by financial results. When Hayes became CEO five years ago, he decided that General Industries was underperforming and that competition in many of the markets would get tougher. He felt that part of the answer was to create a more integrated company that could benefit from joint R&D, from the economies of central services, and from coordinated efforts among related operating units. As part of this thrust, he reorganized the company (see Figure 7-1) into four sectors, each composed of strategically related operating units and headed by an executive vice-president. He also worked to create an effective corporate staff made up of some of the brightest people from the operating units, as well as professionals recruited from staff positions in other companies.

Now, Hayes was wondering whether he had gone too far. The comments about the corporate staff and decision making were troubling and significant, given the increasing demands for quick, decisive action by the sectors. As he reviewed the notes, he wondered how he could best begin to lay out the issues he would need to consider in order to solve this problem.

## INTRODUCTION

Information processing, grouping, and linking provide us with a basic vocabulary for talking about organization design decisions. Before

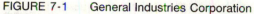

FIGURE 7-1    General Industries Corporation

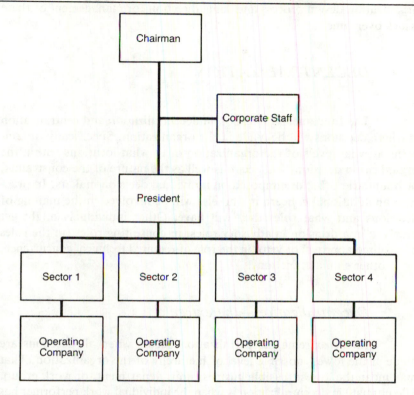

moving on to talk about the process of making design decisions, we will discuss several applied design issues. These are questions that frequently arise in practice; they are often encountered as managers cope with many day-to-day decisions about the structuring of organizations; our goal will be to use the concepts of design that we have been discussing to understand these issues. The first issue will be labeled the **decentralization issue**. The concern here is how to strike the right balance between centralization and decentralization of an organizational structure. The second issue is the **staff and line issue**, or how to design and manage effective staff groups within the context of an operating line organization.

The staff and line and decentralization questions are problematic and omnipresent issues in large organizations. It seems that managers are constantly grappling with either or both of these concerns. Even in the most effective organization, the issues seem to defy solution, and even when some resolution is reached, they keep popping up again. Our objective will be to gain some insight into these important issues and provide some guidance for how to think about the questions in the context of the organization design process and some direction for management of these issues over time.

## DECENTRALIZATION

The fundamental question in decentralization and centralization is where decisions will be made in the organization. Specifically, it concerns at what levels of the organization or at what locations within the organization decisions will occur as well as the nature of the constraints, or boundaries, that are imposed on individual decision makers. In practice, an additional concern is who else will be involved in the making of decisions and what roles they will have. Other individuals might get involved in a decision in advisory roles, in consulting roles, in the roles of required approval or veto, in the role of required technical concurrence, or in other similar functions.

### Decentralization — the extreme

In the extreme, decentralization occurs when all decisions are made at the lowest possible level of hierarchy of the organization. That may mean the lowest feasible business unit, department, or work group. The ultimate in decentralization is when the individual work performer has the discretion to make a wide range of decisions about his or her work. This delegation of decision making is done within only the most minimal of guidelines. For example, in a holding company structure, individual operating companies may only need to meet targets for profit, cash use, or return on assets, while all other decisions are up to the operating company management. Obviously, there are questions of relative level. An organization may decentralize through moving decisions down to a particular level (as in our holding company-operating company example) but then be very centralized in the relationship between the operating company management and its component departments, divisions, or work groups.

Decentralization has a number of distinct advantages. As a design mechanism, it promotes the processing of information among those organizational units, groups, or individuals who are closest to the work being performed. It may also reduce the vertical information-processing requirements placed on the structure, since less information has to move up and down the hierarchy for decisions to be made. In practice, then, decentralization can promote responsiveness to local conditions, be they market

needs, competitive situations, specific product or technological requirements, or human needs. It thus may facilitate the application of relevant
expertise to the work at hand. In addition, decentralization provides the
freedom that is needed to stimulate innovation. For individuals, decentralization may provide the opportunity for more enriched jobs and better internal motivation.

On the other hand, there clearly are disadvantages associated with
decentralization. Three are particularly salient and therefore worth defining: control, coordination, and cost. **Control** involves the effective processing of information so that one level of an organization can ensure that
another (usually lower) level of the organization is acting consistently with
what is required. It usually involves the process of setting goals and standards, monitoring activity or behavior in comparison to those standards
over time, and then taking corrective action (through feedback, incentives,
or direct action) to make sure that the activity stays within acceptable limits of variation from the standard. **Coordination** involves the processing
of information so that various units (usually at the same levels) operate
so that their activities fit together to provide the required consistency of
action across a set of organizational groupings. Coordination may be necessary to achieve internal efficiencies (such as linking sales forecasts with
manufacturing plans) or to provide consistency in relations with the outside world (such as making sure that various customer contact points use
common practices). Decentralization obviously presents problems for both
coordination and control. To the extent that decisions are moved down
in the organization and only minimal boundaries are placed around the
decision maker, there is increased risk of loss of control or decrease in
coordination. A third concern is **cost**, which involves both the direct cost
associated with a design (such as salary costs for staff or location expenses)
as well as the indirect costs (additional time, effort, and management
expense involved in maintaining minimal control over diverse activities).
Decentralization typically has costs associated with it, particularly to the
extent that individual units may develop their own capacities that are
duplicated in other groups.

## Centralization—the extreme

At the other end of the continuum is centralization. In this case,
all decisions of any significance are made at one location in the organization, either by one individual, one group, or one organizational level.
Any decisions that are made at lower levels of the organization are made
only within very specific guidelines, in accordance with detailed decision
rules, or according to standard operating procedures. Situations that

require decisions that do not fit the rules typically are treated as exceptions, which must flow up the hierarchy to the point of central decision making.

The typical advantages of centralization are increased control and the potential to achieve enhanced coordination among units. To the extent that there are economies of scale associated with making certain types of decisions at one point, there also may be direct cost advantages. However, if information is not at the central point, the resulting decision making may be slow, of poor quality, or highly unresponsive to local conditions. In addition, centralization neither leaves room for nor encourages innovation. Finally, some individuals may find such situations demotivating, since much of the autonomy and potential to make decisions is taken out of their jobs.

Obviously, large and complex organizations rarely fit the characteristics of either of these extremes. One cannot make all decisions centrally, since the information-processing capacity of the hierarchy and the individual decision makers would be quickly overloaded. On the other hand, in the absence of any coordination and control, there would be anarchy, and organizations would be unable to act in a coordinated manner to meet the demands of the environment. Therefore, a range of combinations of design features incorporate various elements of centralized and decentralized decision making.

How is this combination of designs done? Typically, choices are made within the range of potential decisions; some decisions are centralized and some are not. When decisions are centralized, it may be through directly designating a central single locus for making the decision or by creating specific decision rules that physically dispersed decisions are still made centrally in a de facto sense. For those decisions that are decentralized, organizations typically create mechanisms to define the scope, focus, and limits of the decentralization. These can be thought of as decision management mechanisms, or devices, to manage the range of alternative decisions to assure that, although decentralized, decisions are made consistent with centralized intentions and goals. Again, this is usually done through a combination of formal organizational arrangements and certain aspects of the informal organization. The formal arrangements that create limits and give focus to decentralized decisions include rules, procedures, specific job/position charters or mandates, controls, training of individuals, and other management processes (regular cycles of goal setting, review, and feedback). The informal mechanisms include socialization of individuals to "the way we do things around here" as well as the development of a specific management style that informally designates the kinds of decisions that can be made autonomously and the kinds that require involvement by the senior management or central location. Thus, any organization is in reality a hybrid, or a combination of different types of decisions, some of which are centralized and some of which are decentralized. In addition, various combinations of formal and informal mechanisms may be employed to achieve the desired limits over decisions that are made.

## Choosing the degree of centralization

As organizations are rarely either fully centralized or decentralized, an important strategic design question is what kinds of decisions are made in a centralized fashion and what decisions are delegated. Several factors are relevant in making these centralization/decentralization decisions:

1. **Organization integration:** To the extent that decisions must be made in an integrated fashion across the organization, these decisions need to be made centrally. Those issues that have strategic importance across the organization must be made centrally; decentralization may lead to fragmentation. For example, resource allocation, technology, or human resource issues that affect the whole organization may be made in a centralized fashion. On the other hand, operational issues that only affect a given division may be made in a decentralized mode. In general, the greater the strategic importance across the organization, the greater the degree of centralization.

2. **Organization crisis:** The greater the need for a rapid, coordinated response to a crisis situation, the greater the need for a centralized decision mode. When integration requirements are substantial and sharply time constrained, it becomes more difficult to utilize decentralized decision practices.

3. **Required control:** As mentioned earlier, the question here is how to assure action consistent with standard, and, in particular, how to maintain control over critical variables. Critical variables are those involving significant risk (such as credit decisions in banks or system design decisions in high-technology organizations). The question is what is strategically important to keep under control because of the consequences of loss of control. When strategically critical issues are defined, limits for central decision making and/or the formal and informal decision management mechanism can be specified.

4. **Economies of scale:** Decentralization frequently means that local groups and units are free to design and build the organization structures they feel are needed to run their own businesses. This frequently promotes the proliferation of various small units

(based on discipline or activity) in each of the decentralized segments of the organization. On the other hand, there may be reasons to assemble a critical mass of resources in one location, or to centralize, because there are economies associated with the scale of a single central group as opposed to many small groups. Examples of economies of scale in organization design might include situations in which there is scarce technical competence, which can best be allocated if taken from a single central source. Analogously, if there is a particular physical resource, such as a computer, machine, or set of specialized tools, it may make sense to supply it through a central point versus replicating it (if financially feasible) or doing without it. Critical mass and scale may also allow for additional subspecialization by discipline or activity within the central group. For example, instead of having one "generalist" technical resource in a decentralized location, scale may allow for a range of specialists who can be justified in a large group and will face sufficient demand across the organization, but who could never be justified within a particular piece of the decentralized organization. To the extent that there are economies of scale possible, centralized structures are advantageous.

5. **Required coordination:** The degree and nature of coordination that is required will influence design decisions about centralization. A key question is how much horizontal coordination is necessary for effective organizational performance. This is very much driven by strategic issues and the basic grouping decisions that are made in designing organizations. Organizations that are grouped by activity (such as functional organizations) frequently are much more interdependent (that is, the different groups are much more dependent on each other to get their core work done) than are organizations grouped by output or user. Thus, grouping may require coordination or may define the limits of autonomous action. As more coordinated activity is required, it becomes more difficult to decentralize. Either decisions must be centralized or other mechanisms must be designed to achieve the required consistency of action across groupings. Clearly, this underscores the need for effective grouping decisions so that the cross-group coordination requirements relating to strategically critical issues will be minimized.

## Decentralization — summary

Organizations selectively structure themselves to centralize and decentralize different types of decisions based on a variety of factors, including coordination and control needs, the need to respond rapidly to an organization-wide crisis, economies of scale, and required integration. Indeed, different types of structures may be created in different parts of a large organization. Just because one part, segment, or function of an organization is centralized does not mean that all similar units must be structured in the same way.

Decentralization at any point in time, therefore, reflects a balance of various formal and informal structures that have been created. One would expect movement over time, if only to help keep the balance. Indeed, as strategic issues, cost considerations, and management personalities change, significant changes in the balance would be expected. The challenge for managers is to recognize the subtlety and sensitivity of that balance and to recognize that an effective balance is achieved through purposeful management of issues, rather than leaving them to drift or to chance.

## STAFF AND LINE

During the discussion of grouping alternatives, the point was made that sometimes different grouping approaches are mixed at one level of the organization. Within any segment of an organization, the primary grouping decisions are made as to how to organize those who are working on the core process of that organizational unit. Core process is the primary task of the organization—those who design, produce, sell, or deliver the organization's products or services.

At the same time, other sets of jobs and people are important to the existence of the organization, even though their work does not involve them as part of the organization's core process. These individuals bring certain functional and/or disciplinary skills, tools, and perspectives to the situation in support of the core process. Frequently, then, groupings are created by activity (i.e., function, discipline, method). These groups have such labels as Planning, Human Resources, Financial Control, and Legal. In practice, those organizational groups that are primarily concerned with the core process tend to be referred to as *line* organizations, while those that are grouped by activity and support the core process are called *staff*.

Staff groups can be thought of as extensions of the management function. They frequently are brought about to aid in coordination and control. In addition, the designation of staff versus line is situational and relative to the nature of the core process. A group that is considered staff in one organization may be line in another setting.

The key issue with the design and structuring of staff units is that those units are frequently viewed as unproductive and are thus seen as overhead. This, obviously, is inherent in their role definition as external to the core work process. Another issue is that problems arise in the relationships among staff and line units at various levels of the hierarchy. Obviously, staff is also linked to the decentralization issue. Staffs, as mechanisms for coordination and control, are devices for achieving de facto centralization. The creation, design, and management of staff groups is thus part of the balancing task of management.

## Why create staff groups?

If there are so many problems associated with staff groups, why are they created in the first place? First, they are created to perform specialized tasks other than the core process. Grouping promotes focus on an issue, and frequently it is necessary to specialize in order to achieve the appropriate degree of emphasis on an issue. Thus, a staff group may be created to provide focus on issues outside of the core process, which would not be addressed effectively in the main grouping scheme. Second, staffs are created to augment the information-processing capacity of the hierarchy for purposes of management decision making and control. A staff is basically an augmentation of the individual manager's capacity to process information, much as an automated information system is a device to augment that capacity. Third, staff groups are created as information-processing devices to aid in the task of coordinating activity among different groups. Staffs may work as interfaces among different groups or may develop and monitor policies and procedures that will assure consistency across groups. They have the technical expertise to process information and the resources to perform the function. Finally, staffs are created where there is a need for expert resources and where (as with any form of centralization) there are economies of scale that justify the creation of a specialized group.

For example, corporate human resource, planning, and/or research and development staff groups develop specialized expertise in their respective areas. These centralized staff groups focus on generic issues in their profession that might impact the firm in the long term and serve as resource bases for professionals working in the divisions. While divisional staffs work on local human resource, planning, and/or technical issues, a central staff coordinates, links, and updates their more local colleagues. Again, staff design is related to the issue of decentralization. Staff groups may be designated at different levels of the hierarchy, and staff groups themselves may be centralized or decentralized.

## Problems associated with staff groups

While there are many benefits associated with the creation of strong and effective staff groups, there is also a considerable number of problems that organizations encounter. Some of the key problems that occur in practice are as follows:

1. **Proliferation and growth:** Once staff groups are created, it may be difficult to bring them to an end. They tend to be self-proliferating. Since the tasks performed are frequently more ambiguous and less observable than that of units in the core process, it may be difficult to identify a completion point and a rationale for doing away with a staff group. Staff groups tend to grow and proliferate over time. Unchecked, they seem to have a tendency to expand.

2. **Direct costs/overhead:** Since staff are not part of the core process, they do not directly contribute the product or service and usually have no productive output or revenue associated with them. Thus, they tend to be seen as overhead. In large organizations, the direct salary costs associated with staff groups at different levels can be staggering.

3. **Indirect costs:** In addition to direct costs, such as salaries, location costs, clerical support, and facilities, there are other indirect costs. Specifically, these are costs in time and effort associated with responding to the demands, requests, and requirements that staff groups pose to line managers. In addition, staff involvement in the decision-making process may have perceived and/or real costs in terms of the quality and timeliness of decisions.

4. **Competition for power:** Organizations are political systems made up of groups that compete for power. Frequently, the formation of staff and line groups with a certain amount of built-in contention and adversary relations creates dysfunctional conflicts and competition for power between the two groups. This competition may have significant direct and indirect costs to the organization.

5. **Internal management and motivation:** Staff groups frequently become difficult to manage internally. Specifically, it may be difficult to effectively manage the staff group to keep people directed, motivated, and satisfied. By definition, the work of staff groups is hard to measure and thus difficult to assess and reward. The role outside of the core process frequently means that there may be limited career opportunities for staff as opposed to line managers.

6. **Bureaucratization:** Staff groups by definition are concerned with the processes or means of getting the work done as opposed to line groups, which may be more focused on the results. In the extremes, staff groups become so concerned about process as opposed to results that they encourage the development of a cul-

ture, climate, and operating style of excessive bureaucratization, in which the means displace the ends. This tends to lead to increased costs, decreased timeliness, and growing frustration.

7. **Building defensive staffs:** The staff problem can feed on itself. Frequently, as staffs grow and place increasing demands on line managers or limit the line managers' actions, the line managers' response is to create their own staff groups to help defend against the invading staff groups. These "defensive" staffs are not designed to aid the management of the core work process but rather as a reaction to aid the manager in fending off the attacks of other staff groups or to help the manager get a proposed action successfully through a staff-infested and -dominated decision-making process. These staffs, in turn, start to create their own requirements and, thus, their own internal management problems, staff-line conflicts, and direct and indirect costs.

## Dealing with the dilemma

This discussion has presented a dilemma. Staffs are a necessary and important element in organizations, and staff groups frequently must be designed as an element of the organizational architecture. On the other hand, a number of significant problems seem to emerge as a natural consequence of the design and creation of staff groups. How do organizations deal with this dilemma?

Again, managers and designers must keep in mind the concept of balance. The creation of staff affects the balance of the organization and the nature of the decision-making processes. Staff can be a tool for managing the decentralization issue, but the design of staff units must be done deliberately. Staff groups are both a consequence and a shaper of management style in the organization. Thus, the design of staff groups should be driven by the same considerations that go into the decentralization issue—by strategic, control, coordination, and integration needs. Thus, the general answer to the question of how organizations manage the staff issue is "with difficulty" and with a clear goal of creating and managing a balance between staff and line concerns.

There is more specific help available, however, through observing how effective organizations manage this issue. In particular, organizations use a number of techniques to keep staff groups from manifesting too many dysfunctional characteristics:

1. **Layering:** One design approach is to limit the number of successive layers of staff through the prohibition of duplicative staffs at successive levels of the organization. In the extreme, if there

is a significant operational staff at one level of the organization (the operating business unit, for example) then no staff (or very limited staff) is allowed at the next level up in the structure (the group/sector/segment level). Layering prevents excessive staff-to-staff interaction across levels. It helps ensure that information will move through the hierarchy in a relatively timely manner.

2. **Rotation:** Some organizations limit the number of permanent or career staff and rotate line employees into staff assignments. This alleviates the internal management problem, helps minimize the conflict that develops, and builds understanding about the different perspectives. In practice, rotational people are used in combination with specialists so that the required technical and professional expertise is combined with a credible and knowledgeable grasp of the organization's core process.

3. **Periodic pruning:** Many organizations have found that, even under the best of conditions, staffs tend to proliferate and that one way to manage this is to plan periodic "pruning" of staff, or reduction in the number of staff groups, positions, and people, usually by moving a significant number of people into line positions.

4. **Clear management processes and roles:** Another aid is to focus on the creation of clearly defined and articulated management processes and roles of groups and individuals within those processes. Staffs tend to create problems most when the management process (particularly the process for goal setting, review, decision making, approval, feedback, and resource allocation) is not well defined. This presents many opportunities for conflict and ambiguity.

5. **Management style/philosophy:** Finally, staff groups are managed through the informal organization—through a management style and philosophy that defines the roles of the staff and the line and then defines the relationships that will exist between them. An example is of a new manager of a major business unit who, in her opening session with her senior management team, stated her view that "staff supports the line, the line is the customer of the staff." Besides articulating this view, she structured her time at work, senior meetings, and day-to-day decision making to be consistent with that view and to manage roles and relationships accordingly.

## Staff—summary

Again the issue is balance, in this case between the needs of the line organization groups to run the core work process and the needs of managers at all levels to have effective staff groups to aid in management through augmenting information processing to achieve desired coordination and control. Managers want and need effective staff groups as part of the organization design, but, at the same time, staff groups create problems. The design of staff groups thus needs to be considered in the context of the information-processing approach as well as in light of the larger organization model we discussed earlier.[1]

## SUMMARY

### Opening case revisited:

Ben Hayes, faced with growing problems at General Industries Corporation, decided to enlist the help of his senior team. He initiated a series of off-site meetings with his president, the four sector heads, and three of the key senior corporate staff officers. The first of these off-site meetings focused on the question of decision making. The group spent several hours listing key decisions on flip charts and identifying whether the decision was made at the operating company, sector, or corporate level. Some of the decisions turned out to be controversial and required a good deal of discussion, and argument, to come to a conclusion. In a few cases, the group was deadlocked, so Ben personally had to make the final call on where a certain decision would be made.

In a second meeting, the role of staff was discussed. The group realized that it could not actually design the staff in detail, but it could provide a general framework for thinking about the role of staff in General Industries. Basic charters were provided for staff at the corporate, sector, and operating company levels. An agreement was reached that to prevent layering and excessive staff-to-staff interactions, the sector heads would have very minimal staffs, drawing on the operating company staff to get specific projects done as appropriate. A goal was also agreed on to cut the number of corporate staff positions significantly, as both a symbolic act and as a means to getting the corporate staff to look critically at the work that it was doing.

What remained was the challenge of turning this design approach into a set of concrete organization recommendations. The senior group knew that it did not have the information or the time to do this in depth. It was then faced with the challenge of how to take a general design "vision" and translate it into a concrete functioning organization design.

This chapter has focused on two applied design issues, which we have called decentralization and staff-line relations. In both, we have applied some of the concepts and terms from the information-processing approach in order to understand the issues, problems, and dilemmas inherent in each of these issues. Two basic implications come through. The first is the need to consider, design in, and manage balance among alternative perspectives. The second is the need, again, to purposefully, deliberately, and systematically approach design decisions, rather than leave them to chance or let historical inertia and drift take hold. These decisions are too important, too complex, and too difficult to treat in that manner. They require the application of appropriate tools on a continuing basis.

## *NOTES*

1. For more detail on line-staff relations and the centralization-decentralization decision, see W. Newman and J. Logan, *Strategy, Policy and Central Management*, (Cincinnati, OH: South-Western, 1981); A. Chandler, *The Visible Hand*, (Cambridge, MA: Harvard University Press, 1977).

# 8

# A Process for Making Design Decisions

**Case:**

Mary Sherman, a vice-president of Great Midwestern Telecommunications Inc., was reflecting on the meeting she had just attended, a half-day session of the top ten officers of the corporation. A variety of topics was discussed, and the last two hours were devoted to a potential reorganization. The company president had talked about the need to restructure the company because of cost concerns, the need to create new business units to take advantage of some opportunities presented by new technology, and a desire to become more responsive to the marketplace.

By and large, the meeting had been a frustrating one. It seemed very difficult to get a firm hold on the topic and come up with solutions. First, everybody talked in generalities; nobody wanted to take a position. Then, all of a sudden, people started drawing charts on pieces of paper and holding them up to show other people. A flip chart was finally brought into the room, and people started jumping up from their seats and running to the easel to draw organization charts. Everyone had a different idea, but the problem seemed to be that everyone was moving in quite different directions with their proposals. Some argued that their approaches would save costs, while others felt that their designs would help develop new managers, while yet others argued for approaches that would move decision making down and out toward the marketplace. There seemed to be little opportunity to focus on the issues and understand the trade-offs. Sherman also noticed that everyone was uncomfortably vague—no one presented a full chart. Sherman guessed that no one wanted to put out a proposal about how many jobs there would be or about who would be in those jobs. Sherman thought, however, that at several points she could see people building jobs for themselves within the structure they proposed.

On the other hand, Sherman thought, there was some good news. Based on what she had heard, the two hours represented a step forward—most of the previous reorganizations had not received that much senior time and attention. Second, she was glad that the senior officers were involved. Word was that in the past the president developed the structure alone and then "tried it out" with a few people through informal and off-the-record discussions. At least we got a chance to talk about it in the open, thought Sherman.

Finally, Sherman realized that the next steps were not clear. The meeting had ended abruptly at 5:30. It was not clear whether additional meetings would occur. Sherman had mixed feelings about another meeting. She was not anxious to repeat this afternoon's session, but she was also uncomfortable with the idea of not having any input to the new organization, particularly since some of her key units and functions might be affected by any redesign.

## INTRODUCTION

As the meeting at Great Midwestern Telecommunications illustrates, making decisions about organization design can be difficult. We all have our own ideas about how to organize. At the same time, there are many variables and options to keep in mind. The thought of juggling all of these different factors is often mind boggling. We frequently tend to fall back on some intuitive or nonsystematic approach, since approaching the problem systematically seems to be an overwhelming challenge.

In this chapter, we will attempt to provide some help for the senior team at Great Midwestern and to other managers or groups of managers at various levels of the organization. In previous chapters, we provided a way of thinking about design decisions (information processing), we described two types of design decisions (strategic and operational), and we gave some thought to key specific design decisions (grouping, structural linking, and management/operational processes). Our purpose here will be to tie together these elements by outlining a very specific, step-by-step process for making decisions about organizational design. In particular, we will work on developing a design decision-making process that uses the various tools but does so in a way that balances strategic and task performance concerns against the concerns related to individuals and the informal organization.

In the first part of this chapter, we will present a general sequence for making organizational design decisions. Within the context of that sequence, we will then focus on strategic organizational design and discuss the logic of decision making for the strategic level. Finally, we will outline a specific series of steps for making strategic design decisions.

## A GENERAL SEQUENCE FOR MAKING DESIGN DECISIONS

In general, a full cycle of organization design work involves four major phases of activity (see Figure 8-1). The first phase is **preliminary analysis**. Organization design decision making is a special case of the organizational problem-analysis and problem-solving model presented in Chapter 2 as part of the discussion of the congruence model. The congruence model leads, indeed pushes, us to understand the current functioning of the organization, to understand the nature of the problems, and to understand what factors are causing those problems before starting to work on the development of solutions. The message is clear that treatment without diagnosis, or solutions in search of problems, can lead the manager into trouble. Organization redesign is a solution. Therefore, prior to working on the construction of a solution, it is critical to do the necessary diagnosis through data collection and analysis.

Data collection and analysis should be done in the preliminary analysis phase. While the data to be collected and examined should include a broad range of information, such as suggested by the congruence model, three types of data are absolutely critical for design. First, data need to be assembled concerning the strategy of the organization. It is impossible to make informed design decisions in the absence of definitive strategy statements (as opposed to broad generalizations that say that the organization will attempt to do everything and be good at it). Second, there must be at least minimal data about the nature of the organization's work. This should include: what are the major work flows or elements of the work; how do they move through the current organization; and what are the major requirements of or constraints on that work flow as imposed by strategy, the environment, and technology. Third, there needs to be some identification of current problems (and ideally, causes) to which the

FIGURE 8-1     A General Sequence for Organizational Design

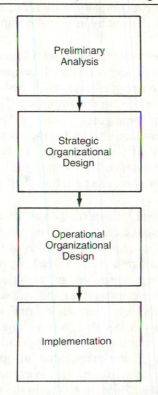

design should be responsive. Obviously, some form of model-driven inquiry is desirable, particularly using a model that compels the designer to identify individual and informal organization factors that might impact the design (or be influenced by it).

The second phase of activity is **strategic organizational design**. Strategy should be the fundamental, albeit clearly not the only, factor driving the basic architecture of the organization. As discussed earlier, designing at the operational level before redesigning at the strategic level can create significant problems. The strategic organizational design (or at least a test of whether strategic redesign is needed) must be done first so that it can provide a context, or limits within which the operational design work can be done.

Strategic organizational design involves decisions on the basic shape of the organization. In the language of the information-processing model, it involves an analysis of broad information-processing requirements and decision making regarding grouping and structural linking. It usually focuses on the top two to four levels of the organization being designed (which could be a company, a division, or a department). It is driven by strategy and balanced by informal organization and individual concerns.

The third phase involves **operational organizational design** decisions. Not every strategic organizational design requires operational design, but many do. Some redesigns may involve just the movement of groups, without much impact on the work flows, jobs, or control mechanisms within or among those groups. Most of the time, however, strategic design decisions have implications for the operational design of units. However, it may not be of universal impact. After the strategic design work is completed, some parts of the organization may need operational design work, while other parts can be left as they are or with only minor modifications.

Operational design focuses on the various management and operational processes of the organization, as well as on some basic grouping and structural linking decisions at lower levels of the organization (these are usually called *job design* at those levels). Operational design occurs within the context of the strategic design, with the primary focus on the flow of work through the organization and on building the mechanisms to facilitate the performance of that work, consistent with strategy. The design work in this phase is usually driven by one or more current operational concerns. For example, in some operational designs, the key concern is cost or cost effectiveness, while in other situations it is the maximization of employee involvement. An example would be the operational design process developed at AT&T in the mid-to-late 1970s. The approach made use of the Hackman-Oldham job design model[1] and had the explicit goal of creating more meaningful jobs — jobs that would lead to higher levels of internal motivation — in addition to building a cost-effective task-performing work system.

As we have said before, we will not spend much time in this book discussing the details of operational design. There is a number of different approaches currently being used in organizations for making operational design decisions.

The fourth phase of designing is **implementation**. One common error is the assumption that the design work is complete once the charts are finished or the design document is produced. If the goal of design is to contribute to increased organizational effectiveness, then a design sequence has not been completed until the design is installed and implemented. An organization redesign of any significant size, however, constitutes a major change. The questions of implementation are not trivial. Thus, in the fourth phase, the designer needs to think carefully about the potential issues of implementation, plan the implementation of the design, and then go ahead with the implementation, monitoring progress along the way. Given the importance of this phase, we will discuss the issues of implementation in much greater detail in Chapter 10.

## STRATEGIC ORGANIZATION DESIGN — THE LOGIC

Within the general design sequence, strategic organizational design is critical because it is where the basic shape and configuration of the organization is decided. Before working through the specific steps of strategic design, it is important to understand the logic that underlies the decision process. In Figure 8-2, the logic of the strategic design process is represented graphically. At the top of the diagram, two factors feed into the strategic design process. First is the particular problem, pain, need, or opportunity that has precipitated the design work. Second should be the data assembled and the analysis done as a result of the preliminary analysis phase.

Within strategic organization design, there are four sets of activities (we will shortly break these down into a set of more detailed specific decision steps). The basic goal of the four activities is to first identify the requirements for the design and then generate a broad number of design alternatives. These alternatives are then tested, evaluated, modified, and refined. At each step, some designs are discarded so that at the end of the process, the designers have one design (and potentially some backup designs).

In the design criteria activities, the precipitating need and the preliminary analysis data are used to write a series of statements about what the new organization design should accomplish. These statements are then used as benchmarks, or evaluation criteria. Next, the basic grouping decisions are made. A number of grouping alternatives are generated and then evaluated. Third, the structural linking decisions are made for each of the grouping alternatives that are still "alive." Here again, some alternatives are combined and some eliminated. Finally, an impact analysis is done. The grouping/structural linking designs are examined for their impact or potential fit with the other aspects of the organization (individual and informal organization). Again assessments, changes, and modifications are made. Coming out of impact analysis, a final design recommendation/choice is made. At the same time, the impact analysis yields information that will be useful in the subsequent design phases — operational design and implementation.

The process, then, starts by creating designs driven primarily by

FIGURE 8-2     The Logic of the Strategic Organization Design Process

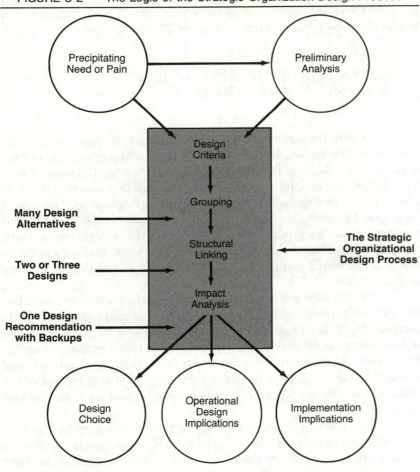

strategic, task, and problem-solving concerns. Through the process, the range of alternatives is narrowed, based on strategy-driven criteria. During the latter part of the process, the individual and informal organization perspectives are used to modify designs, to aid in the choice of designs, and to identify implications for operational design and implementation. Typically, one might come into impact analysis with two or three design options, each of which is comparable in fit with the strategy and task. The final decision is then made on the basis of the impact analysis results. Thus, the process builds into the decision-making steps, the concept of balance that we have been discussing.

# STRATEGIC ORGANIZATION DESIGN— SPECIFIC DECISION-MAKING STEPS

The logic of strategic organization has been used in practice, through the development of a process for making design decisions that includes ten specific steps of analysis and decision making (see Figure 8-3). These steps are as follows:

1. **Generate design criteria.** The first step is to turn the results of the preliminary analysis into a set of concrete and usable criteria for both directing and assessing the design efforts. Design criteria are statements that describe, in ideal terms, those functions that the organization design should perform. Criteria statements include an action verb; they state that the design should *facilitate, promote, encourage, motivate,* or *provide for.* Each design criteria statement can be thought of as the completion of a sentence that starts: "The organization design should. . . . "

Design criteria statements are developed from information gathered in the preliminary analysis phase, keeping in mind the specific precipitating need, pain, or challenge that initiated the design work. There are four possible sources of information to guide the development of design criteria:

a. Strategy—the business strategy of the unit(s) being designed; in particular information about markets, products/services, or the key competitive basis or proposed distinctive competence of the organization.

b. Task—the basic characteristics of the major flows of work through the organization needed to execute the strategy.

c. Diagnosis—information about current problems the organization is facing (with causes) to which the new design should respond.

d. Other—other information about possible constraints or demands on the designs that are being developed.

During this step, design criteria are written and refined. In addition, they are rated for relative importance in the design decision making. The criteria are then written down for use in the subsequent decision-making steps.

It is difficult to overestimate the importance of the design criteria. As we will see, they drive the entire design decision-making process and serve as the basic device linking design decisions

FIGURE 8-3     Strategic Organization Design Process:
               Specific Decision-Making Steps

| Step | Objective |
| --- | --- |
| 1. Generate design criteria | Create a series of statements that can serve as criteria for assessing different designs. |
| 2. Generate grouping alternatives | Create a large number of different grouping alternatives designed to meet the design criteria. |
| 3. Evaluate grouping alternatives | Assess grouping alternatives in terms of design criteria; eliminate, modify, and refine alternatives. |
| 4. Identify coordination requirements | For each grouping alternative, identify the information-processing needs, working from the design criteria. |
| 5. Generate structural linking mechanisms | For each grouping alternative, create a set of structural linking mechanisms that will be responsive to the coordination requirements and will enhance the extent to which the design meets the design criteria. |
| 6. Evaluate structural linking mechanisms | Assess each alternative in terms of the design criteria; eliminate, modify, and refine alternatives. Combine alternatives if necessary. |
| 7. Conduct impact analysis | Assess each surviving design alternative in terms of predicted impact on or fit with other organizational components. |
| 8. Refine and eliminate designs | Based on the impact analysis, eliminate designs, resulting in a first choice design recommendation, and refine designs as appropriate. |
| 9. Identify issues for operational design | Based on impact analysis, identify where operational design needs to be done and issues to be addressed by the design. |
| 10. Identify issues for implementation | Based on impact analysis, identify key issues to be considered in planning implementation of the design. |

to strategy and to the other factors identified in the preliminary analysis.

2. **Generate grouping alternatives.** The next step is to create a number of potential grouping alternatives for the organization being designed. This activity should make use of the various grouping options and combinations available to managers (review Chapter 5). The objective is to develop a number of significantly different grouping alternatives. The emphasis here is on creativity; not being constrained by questions of implementation, feasi-

bility or practicality; and not being limited by the current grouping of the organization. This group-alternative step is equivalent to brainstorming in many classical problem-solving routines. The objective is to be creative and produce a quantity of different designs. Later in the process, the designs can be evaluated, eliminated, or refined. Typically, at this stage, anywhere from five to fifteen different designs might be created, depending on the situation.

3. **Evaluate grouping alternatives.** The various grouping alternatives generated are then assessed by rating them on the list of design criteria. Frequently this is done on a numerical scale (such as a 1–5 effectiveness scale). The objective is first to get a sense of the relative strengths and weaknesses of each design and thus the trade-offs involved in each. Typically during this phase of assessment, features from different designs are combined and new ideas sometimes develop. The objective is to use the ratings to refine, combine, and eliminate designs. However, the designer should still attempt to keep a number (three at the minimum) of different designs alive to take into the next step. Thus, when this step is completed there should be several designs "on the table" that are significantly different, and for each, there should be a written record of the ratings of the effectiveness of the design, in terms of the original set of design criteria.

4. **Identify coordination requirements.** Grouping creates a number of "designs," but in reality they are just sets of grouping alternatives, although sometimes they include some of the basic reporting relationships — the groups are placed in a structural hierarchy. In step 4, the task is to assess the key information-processing requirements that would exist among the different groups in each alternative, keeping in mind the strategy, the nature of the task, and other factors as reflected in the design criteria. Thus, the coordination requirements include two basic elements:

a. the between group information-processing requirements.
b. the "leftover" design criteria — i.e., those criteria on which the particular grouping alternative scored low.

5. **Generate structural linking alternatives.** For each grouping alternative on the table, the next step is to generate or design structural linking mechanisms that will be responsive to the coordination requirements identified in step 4. Despite the fact that one might consider a number of alternative linking mechanisms for each grouping alternative, in practice, designers usually seem to be comfortable with developing only one set of structural link-

ages for each of the grouping alternatives, although different alternatives may be considered in the development of that set of structural linkages. Again, the goal is to design structural linkages that will be responsive to the coordination requirements and thus make each design more effective in total.

6. **Evaluate structural linking mechanisms.** The designer now has a set of grouping/structural linking alternatives on the table. The next step is to assess those alternatives in light of the basic design criteria and any additional coordination requirements that were identified in step 4. Ratings are made on paper of each design, and here again, features of different designs are frequently combined. The assessment includes modification, refinement, and elimination of designs. It should be noted that frequently the elimination occurs implicitly in step 5, where the designer finds that it is just too difficult, problematic, or costly to link a certain set of groups.

As a result of this step in the process, the designer should now have a number of designs (a minimum of two, but usually no more than four), and each design should have ratings committed to paper of how well it meets the different design criteria.

7. **Conduct impact analysis.** The basic balancing work of design decision making is done in impact analysis. Depending on the design criteria, political, individual, or cultural issues may be reflected in the designs developed through step 6. In addition, the designer is not working in a vacuum but indeed should be aware of many of these issues as he or she works through the design steps. Even so, to date the design has been primarily driven by strategic and task concerns. If the work has been done effectively in the previous steps, the designer should be able to go into impact analysis with a number of designs, which, while different, meet the strategic and task-driven design criteria. This is what some call the *feasible set* of designs. The identification of this feasible set of organization designs is strategy driven, but the final modifications and choices from that set are driven by other concerns (individual, informal organization, historical).

The impact analysis is done by asking a number of questions that lead to an assessment of the potential impact of the design (see Figure 8-4 for a listing of basic impact analysis questions). The questions focus on the potential consequences associated with the choice of this particular design alternative. Questions focus on the individual and informal organization components, but they also are frequently asked about certain input-related factors, cost, and other issues that may have been noted during the other steps of the process. The objective is to provide

FIGURE 8-4     Key Impact Analysis Questions

*Individuals*
— To what extent does the design decrease the quality of fit between the requirements of the work and the capacities of individuals?
— To what extent does the design require managerial skills, talents, or experience that is not currently present?
— To what extent does the design limit or decrease opportunities to meet individual needs?
— To what extent does the design limit or decrease the ability to motivate needed behavior?

*Informal Organization*
— To what extent does the design conflict with the following factors:
  — current leadership style?
  — current organizational culture (values and beliefs)?
  — current communications and influence patterns?
  — other informal arrangements or aspects of the informal organization?

*Input*
— To what extent does the design pose problems in relation with the outside environment?
— To what extent will the design require significant additions to or reallocations of human, capital, plant, technological, or other resources?
— To what extent will the design create problems because of past practices?

*Cost*
— To what extent will the implementation of the design require incurring additional costs (direct or indirect)?

both a numerical rating of the extent of impact (positive or negative impact) and specific written descriptions of the predicted impact. In terms of the general congruence model, we are placing a new set of design features in the organizational arrangements box in the model diagram and identifying this impact in terms of fit. In this step, we are attempting to simulate the consequences of design choice in place of discovering them through trial and error.

The results of the impact analysis for each design against the total list of design criteria are pulled together. For each impact area, the designer is asked to list possible implications of the impact area for either operational design or implementation. The impact analysis is critical because it pulls together the earlier analysis steps, focuses the designer on questions of balance, and provides data for the remaining three steps.

8. **Refine and eliminate designs.** Following impact analysis, the designer examines the designs, makes any refinements or modifications implied by the impact analysis, and eliminates problem-

atic designs. This typically leaves one design that is a first choice, although at least one backup alternative should be identified, depending on the final decision-making, approval, or implementation process. For each design, then, there should be a description of its major features, as well as a written analysis of the relative strengths and weaknesses of the design (ratings on the design criteria) and its potential impact on the other components of the organization.

9. **Identify issues for operational design.** Next, the designer needs to pose and then answer the question of what operational design work will be necessary in order to make the new strategic design function effectively. In a few cases, there may be little or no operational design work indicated, while in the other extreme, the entire organization must be worked through an operational design. Usually it is somewhere in between. Parts of the organization may not need to be redesigned operationally (except for minor modifications), while other parts will need significant operational redesign. The key here is an examination of the original design criteria (which ones were not met and therefore require a response through operational design) as well as the implications for operational design identified in the impact analysis. Finally, as a check, the designer should spend some time tracing how key work would flow through the new organization to reveal where the current operational structures or processes may break down.

In practice, operational design may not be a separate activity but rather included as part of the job of those who are charged with managing the implementation of the design. There is nothing wrong with that, as long as that decision is made deliberately and the resources needed for an adequate operational design process are made available.

10. **Identify issues for implementation.** Finally, the designer needs to gather information about the possible issues to be encountered in implementing the design. Again, the primary source is the impact analysis, in which implications for implementation were noted. These data are important, for they will serve as guiding input for those who are responsible for managing the implementation (see Chapter 10).

While not an explicit, formal step in strategic organizational design, it frequently is useful to pull together the completed analyses into a written design document. This is particularly critical in a large redesign, where others will be involved in the operational design and implementation, since they will benefit greatly from access to the data generated during the strategic design process. If the strategic organizational design steps are followed, the written material will basically be produced as part of the work (through flip charts, forms, or written pages), and thus the design document merely involves writing a brief narrative around those key pieces of paper.

## A FINAL QUESTION: WHO DOES THE STRATEGIC DESIGN?

The description of the strategic organization design steps has been intentionally vague as to the identity of "the designer." In practice, the designer may be various people or sets of people. In some cases, the designer is the chief operating officer or manager of the unit involved, working alone or with help. In other cases, it may be the manager and one or two others as in the Landis & Co. case in Chapter 2. In some situations, there is a design team composed of people in various positions, including people who are subject-matter experts on different aspects of the organization — for example, strategic planning and human resources. In yet other cases, the senior management team of the unit serves as the design team.

The choice of designer or design team members clearly is influenced by a number of factors, including the nature of the organizational climate; the leadership style of the senior manager; the relationships among the individuals involved; and the knowledge, skills, or motivation of individuals. One rule, however, has developed from experience with this process: those who will be responsible for implementing the design (or managing the organization designed) must be involved in the design. The strategic design responsibility (as opposed to operational design) does not seem to be delegated easily. When it is delegated, the designs are rarely implemented or last minute changes are made in a haphazard manner, which violates all of the assumptions built into the decision-making process. Thus, it is strongly recommended that managers be involved in designs and that the role of consultants should be to help managers make design decisions, not to develop design recommendations without significant managerial involvement.

## SUMMARY

**Opening case revisited:**

Mary Sherman found the opportunity to sit down with the CEO of Great Midwestern Telecommunications and to argue for a different approach for going about the restructuring of the company. Sherman proposed the creation of a design team, a set of people who would be assigned the task of coming up with a number of alternative designs for the company. This team would be made up of people one and two levels below the most senior team (direct reports to the CEO), and care would be taken to find people who had strong reputations as good managers, who knew the business, who were not very political-minded, and who were not afraid to deal directly with tough issues. This team, working with an outside consultant, would systematically work through a process of strategic organization design and develop some different design alternatives to present to the senior group.

At the same time, Sherman proposed, the senior team would spend some time on the design issue. It would not do the actual designing — some of the people in the senior group were just too involved to be constructive and objectives in the course of putting together the design. On the other hand, the senior group could work to create design criteria for the design team to use. As "customers" of the design team, they did not have to be involved in building the product, but they did have to be involved in defining the requirements that a quality product would have to meet. The design team chairman also would meet frequently with the senior team to provide regular updates on progress and to get decisions from the senior team (such as which grouping alternatives to pursue) as needed.

The CEO responded positively to Sherman's suggestion. He saw in this approach a method for getting participation in the restructuring but without the confusion and frustration that had characterized the first meeting. He told Sherman that this new approach would be proposed at the next senior team meeting.

We have outlined a general approach, a logical sequence, and finally, a process comprising specific steps for making organization design decisions. The process is constructed to be logical, systematic, and facilitative of balancing different concerns and making informed trade-offs.

In the remaining chapters, we will focus on a number of issues important for those who are considering using this approach to organization design. Throughout the book, we have referred to the informal organization as a key element of design decision making. In Chapter 9, we will focus in more depth on the informal organization through a discussion of a model of organizational cultures and then relate that model to organization design decisions. In Chapter 10, we will concentrate on the larger question of implementation and discuss an approach and some guidelines for effectively managing the implementation of new organization designs. In Chapter 11, we will return to a discussion of organizations over time and point out when to anticipate the need for significant redesign.

## *NOTES*

1. R. Hackman and G. Oldham, *Work Re-design*, (Reading, MA: Addison-Wesley, 1980); M. Hanlon, D. Nadler, and D. Gladstein, *Attempting Work Reform*, (New York: Wiley, 1982).

# 9

# Strategic Linking and the Informal Organization: Managing Organization Cultures

**Cases:**

Jean Shaeffer at Federal Engineering announced her new systems organization and the new system manager. While the structure was in place to achieve coordination, Shaeffer saw no behavioral changes in her organization. The fiefdoms and opposing groups that developed over the years seemed unwilling or incapable of working together on systems products.

Roger Laffer's technology transfer board was introduced by the CEO and was met with widespread approval, yet the mechanics of the technology transfer board seemed to be causing more problems than Laffer expected. The different product divisions had their unique priorities and fought with each other as to who would get what project, who would contribute what resources, and which division would get additional resources. The technology transfer board floundered.

Allen Roberts is announced as the new president for the Consumer Products Corporation, a major autonomous operating company that is part of a larger conglomerate. Within a few weeks after coming on the job, Roberts initiates a major restructuring of the organization to support the new strategic thrusts that he has developed. In the following months, however, Roberts begins to realize that while the organization structure fits with his strategic vision, the company's mediocre performance is matched by a feeling of comfort with mediocrity among senior management members. As one company officer states, "We've been happy with a 'gentleman's C.' It's acceptable to do poorly as long as one does it with style." Roberts starts to ponder how he is going to change this style of operating.

These vignettes suggest that strategic linking alone is not sufficient to achieve coordination between interdependent units. While structural linking is a necessary condition for effective coordination, it must be bolstered with an informal organization that can deal with all of the complexities that formal organizations ignore (review Chapter 6; see Figure 9-1). The more complex the work interdependence, the greater the importance of a healthy informal organization to provide social glue to reinforce structural linking. As with strategic grouping and structural linking, management must shape the informal organization at different levels of analysis. This chapter builds on our work in strategic grouping and linking and discusses shaping organizational culture as an important complement to formal strategic linking. We discuss organizational culture and its components, the effects of culture on behavior, and levers for shaping cultures within complex organizations.

## BACKGROUND AND ASSUMPTIONS

In each of the vignettes that opened this chapter, an unknown factor has played an important role in shaping the destinies of these organizations. Both managers and students of organization have struggled for some time to comprehend the nature of the undercurrents that ebb and flow in organizational life. Early researchers tended to talk about the informal organization; we have built on research on the informal organization and have included it in our organizational model (see Chapter 2). Others have developed the ideas of organization climate, while more recently, there has been increasing use of the term *organizational culture* to describe the implicit and emergent patterns of behavior, activities, and emotions that characterize life in organizations.[1]

Whatever its label, the idea of this softer side of organizations is alluring. The fantasy is of some magic force, some secret ingredient, or some mystical "glue" that brings together all of the people in an organization in a sense of shared purpose, commitment, and direction. Part of the fascination with Japanese organizations, for example, has been based on the view that they have figured out how to develop this secret ingredient and make it work for them.

FIGURE 9-1     Strategic Linking: Designing Formal Structures and Cultures
               for Coordination

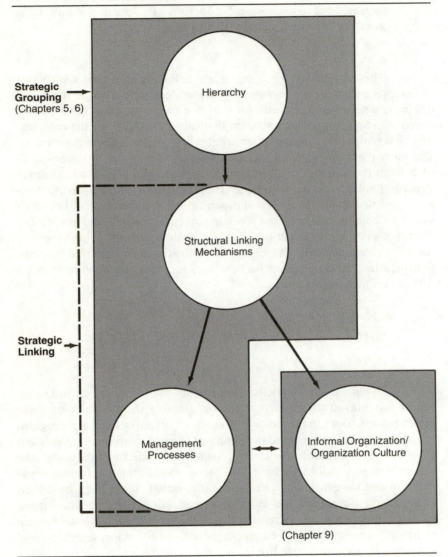

Strategic
Grouping
(Chapters 5, 6)

Hierarchy

Structural Linking
Mechanisms

Strategic
Linking

Management
Processes

Informal Organization/
Organization Culture

(Chapter 9)

While much has been written about culture in organizations, little work has been done to define it in terms complex enough to capture
the intricacies and subtlety of the phenomenon but simple enough to be
used by managers in their efforts to understand and shape organizational
cultures. This chapter is an attempt to do that task. We build on ideas pre-

sented in Chapter 2 in defining a workable and pragmatic view of what culture is and how cultures are developed in organizations. Our purpose is to better understand organizational cultures as tools in service of strategic linking.

The foundation of any culture is made up of a set of *core values* and/or *core beliefs*. Core values are statements about what is good (and by implication, what is not good) in an organization. Core values can define the goodness or badness of behaviors (e.g., employee participation is good) as well as different traits, or characteristics (e.g., innovation and creativity is valued). For example, at IBM, the core values are (1) respect for the individual, (2) customer service, and (3) individual excellence. Beliefs, on the other hand, are views about how the world works. Beliefs describe people's perceptions of the relations between action and their consequences. Beliefs can be thought of as if-then relationships. For example, a core belief at IBM is that attention to customer service and excellence will lead to market success. At Tandem Computer, the core values of quality, personal excellence, and teamwork are associated with the belief that attending to these core values will, in turn, assure both organizational and personal growth.

A second aspect of culture is that the values and beliefs are shared. Culture involves *a set of values, beliefs, and norms* (i.e., expected behaviors) *that are held in common by people in a group*. Thus, culture is defined by the values that people hold jointly and the beliefs that they develop together over time.

Third, culture provides organization members with an *integrated image* of their organization. Core values, beliefs, and norms are not random. Rather, they fit together to form a larger picture of the organization and of how it should work. The set of values, beliefs, and norms provides a gestalt that helps individuals define their own role and helps focus individual and group behavior. In our "gentleman's C" example, the culture includes the values (style is good), the beliefs (you have to look good to get ahead), and the associated behaviors—how to dress, act, speak, make decisions, and so on. Similarly, Tracy Kidder's discussion of Tom West's group at Data General describes a set of core values (meet the deadline at all costs, teamwork, no pats on the back), core beliefs (if we win we can design the next machine), and appropriate behaviors (e.g., long hours, work weekends).[2]

Finally, culture appears to be a *persistent phenomenon*. Once created, a unit's culture persists; it is resistant to change. This social inertia has both positive and negative implications. For example, the core values and beliefs at AT&T around universal, low-cost service are rooted in seventy years of history. The "Ma Bell" culture, once the source of enormous energy, may well hinder the new AT&T as it tries to develop a more competitive organizational culture.

Culture, then, can be defined as the social glue that bonds individuals together. It is the set of core ideas, beliefs, values, and norms which individuals build and transmit over time. The longer a particular culture is reinforced, the more persistent the culture becomes. These social forces take on a life of their own and represent a powerful social force for stability.

## DIMENSIONS OF CULTURE

We can look more deeply at corporate culture by tracking core values, norms, climate, and key roles. While we will refer to corporate culture, keep in mind that organizations are made up of a set of distinct cultures. Just as strategic grouping and structural linking are issues at multiple levels of analysis, so too is the issue of diagnosing and shaping organizational cultures.

### Core values and beliefs

Core values and beliefs define what members of the organization believe in, what is good and bad, what members hold to be true and important. Core values and beliefs provide the guiding assumptions, or axioms, for social relations in an organization. For example, from the Kingsbury Agreement of 1913 to the mid-1970's, universal service was a core value at AT&T. High-quality service was the driving principle throughout the Bell System. This core value was reflected in a myriad of ways, from its service-oriented measurement system to its corporate seal (which had the words "universal service" in it). At General Radio, an important scientific instrument firm, the core values centered around the importance of engineering ("the engineer is king here") and high-quality/high-priced scientific instruments ("we are the Cadillac of the instrument industry"). At Federal Engineering, the core values centered on technological excellence, divisional independence, and autonomy. These core values flew in the face of the need for cooperation and synthesis to get into the systems business.

Other core values might be related to how a firm views its customers (at IBM, the customer is king), its people (Tandem and ARCO emphasize their commitment to human resources), its competition ("the bastards say welcome," according to Data General), its communities (CDC's huge corporate commitment to those communities in which it operates), and its technologies (DEC's and Hewlett-Packard's emphasis on technological excellence) (see Figure 9-2).

FIGURE 9-2    Dimensions of Organizational Culture

| | |
|---|---|
| **Core Values or Beliefs Regarding:** | **Organization Climate Norms Regarding:** |
| — Competition | — Commitment |
| — Technology | — Work standards |
| — Employees | — Recognition |
| — Self-Image | — Teamwork |
| — External groups | |
| — Critical functions | |
| **Norms, or Expected Behaviors:** | **Key Roles:** |
| — Dress code | — Idea generators |
| — Language | — Champions/entrepreneurs |
| — Working hours | — Boundary spanners |
| — Work standards | — Sponsors or mentors |
| — Reward contingencies | |
| — Conflict resolution patterns | |
| — Boss-subordinate relations | |

While core values are ephemeral and hard to pin down, they can be diagnosed. A useful indicator of core values and beliefs is the stories, heroes, myths, and rituals that persist in all organizations. Each myth, hero, story, or saga has a clear message about what the organization holds important. For example, at AT&T the folk hero Angus McDonald drives out in a blinding snowstorm to fix the phone service in an elderly widow's home. McDonald epitomized the old AT&T zeal for universal, low-cost, high-quality service. At Citibank, the stories and myths surrounding John Reed's turnaround of the back office in the early 1970s convey the Citibank values of aggressiveness, innovation, and intensity in service of profits. Similarly, the stories that the president of a high-tech organization still has an office and actually spends time in the laboratory conveys information about the importance of technology in this firm and of the importance of each person as a contributor.

## Norms and organization climate

Values have no behavioral referent and cannot be proven right or wrong. For example, "customer is king" and "we are a technology driven firm" convey core values but have no direct behavioral consequences. It is not clear how one might demonstrate adherence to any one value. Whereas core values have no clear behavioral referents, norms do. Norms elaborate and make concrete a unit's core values. Norms are clearly specified expected behaviors, such that if they are violated, then the individual is sanctioned by the group. Norms always arise in social settings. If core values are clear, a set of norms evolves consistent with those core values. However, if core values are ambiguous, then a range of inconsistent or diffuse norms will evolve.

Norms guide all aspects of organizational life. Norms define broad issues, such as "how things get done here," "what it takes to get ahead," and "how we treat our employees," to more mundane matters, such as what is appropriate dress, humor, and language; how decisions really get made; who gets what parking space; who eats with whom; what is a fair day's pay; when to show up at work; how late to work; how to deal with conflict, and so on. Groups enforce their norms and sanction deviants. Furthermore, groups recruit, socialize, and train new members so they carry on the set of traditions, which are, in turn, bolstered by an overarching set of core values (review Figure 9-2).

Organizations vary enormously in their normative order. These differences are driven by differences in core values. Some business schools, for example, value research and contribution to core disciplines. Faculty reward each other for independent research, publication, and professional prestige and not for teaching, student attention, collaboration, or contact with organizations. Other business schools value practical application, teaching, and student involvement. Neither normative order is better than the other. They both produce excellent students, although the schools are driven by fundamentally different core values.

Norms regarding how one treats senior executives also convey core values. In a bank, for example, when employees go to see the president they always put on their suit jackets and button the jacket before entering the office. In contrast, in a high-technology firm, people take off their jackets before seeing the president, who doesn't wear a jacket. There are no written rules in either situation, but everyone knows what you are supposed to do when you see the president. These norms reflect different values: button-up high-level customer contact versus "shirtsleeves, let's get down to work and dispense with formalities."

Whereas norms define expected behavior over any number of situations, the work on organizational climate focuses on a set of specific norms:

1. *Commitment* refers to how strongly individuals are expected to be dedicated to their unit's achievements. Commitment can vary from substantial to minimal.

2. *Standards* reflect the extent to which groups expect an emphasis on high versus mediocre performance standards.

3. *Recognition* reflects the extent to which people feel that they should recognize and reward excellence versus situations in which everyone expects to be rewarded equally.

4. *Teamwork* reflects the degree to which individuals value and support collaboration, teamwork, and collegeality. Whereas some organizations value teamwork, others value individual entrepreneurship.

While these dimensions of organizational climate tap only a particular set of norms, they are clearly related to the tone, or feel, of an organization. Those organizations in which individual commitment and personal standards are expected to be low and in which all are expected to be rewarded equally will most likely feel like a low-energy, low-performance organization (review Figure 9-2).

Norms exist in all organizations at all times. They vary, however, in intensity and consistency. Whereas some organizations value teamwork, high standards, and high commitment, others informally reward mediocre standards, indifferent commitment, and individual independence. Core values and beliefs provide the underlying energy for norms and organization climate to evolve. Organizations with a clear set of core values will have a consistent, overlapping, and intense set of norms, while those organizations with diffuse and/or inconsistent core values will have a vague and inconsistent set of norms. For example, in a mid-sized advertising agency, the president's shift in espoused values from "we are a creative boutique" to "we are creating inexpensive standard copy" resulted in a set of inconsistent norms in the agency and in confusion and creative paralysis. Norms, then, always arise in social settings. If expected behaviors are not shaped by an overarching set of values and/or beliefs, then norms and organization climate will evolve in their own idiosyncratic fashion (see Figure 9-3).

In sum, whereas core values are reflected in sometimes vague and/or ephemeral statements, norms are a set of expected behaviors that guide and direct all aspects of life in organizations. Norms are shaped and ordered by core values. If these core values are absent or inconsistent, norms will evolve chaotically. Groups sanction deviants and ensure that recruits are quickly socialized. Norms can be diagnosed simply by observing patterns of behavior over time and asking members how and why their organizations operate as they do.

## Key roles

Norms and values create a normative order, which guides behavior and has an important impact on strategic linking. Beyond norms and values, several key functions must also be accomplished to achieve strategic linking in complex organizations. **Idea generating and synthesis**

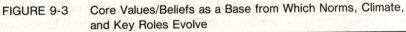

FIGURE 9-3     Core Values/Beliefs as a Base from Which Norms, Climate, and Key Roles Evolve

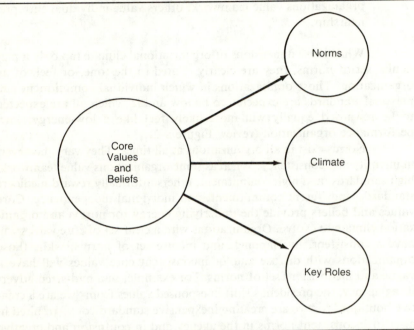

across disciplines or departments; **championing products, ideas, or ventures** between areas; **boundary spanning,** or linking disparate areas together; and **sponsoring projects and ideas** across organizational boundaries are all vital linking functions that must evolve out of the organization's informal organization.[3]

These critical linking functions cannot be formalized; they cannot be made part of the organization's structure or systems. Indeed, when organizations have attempted to formalize these functions, they have tended to disappear. Further, the exercise of these functions is not equally distributed within organizations. Research on critical functions finds that no more than 15 percent of individuals within an organization perform these key functions. Several key informal roles can be identified to fulfill the linking functions identified above:

1. Idea generators: those few individuals who synthesize ideas and insights from distinct areas in a creative fashion.

2. Champions: individuals who cause creative ideas (which they may or may not create) to happen. These individuals sell ideas, take risks, and get resources for their project or "cause."

3. Gatekeepers or boundary spanners: individuals who are able to effectively link their more local colleagues to important information outside the organization or business unit.

4. Sponsors: more senior levels of an organization who provide informal support, resources, and protection for atypical projects or ideas.

While these informal roles cannot be formalized, they can be encouraged, developed, and grown. For example, after an R&D director tried unsuccessfully to appoint gatekeepers, she instead identified key contributors and provided those individuals with increased travel support and better access to the computer, and she involved them more in interorganizational teams and task forces. Further, she explicitly rewarded and encouraged her key contributors so that they felt recognized for accomplishing these several linking functions.

These critical roles have an important, although informal, impact on linking. Without idea generators, the quality of the collaboration between areas will be relatively low; without champions, joint efforts will not take off; without gatekeepers, the units will not be able to effectively take advantage of in-house or external expertise; and without sponsors, inherent organizational resistance will impede the linking process.

As with norms and values, critical roles can be assessed by either observation or limited interviewing. Once these roles are defined, managers usually know exactly who fills these roles and which roles are not filled. These roles must be shaped, developed, and rewarded by managers so that individuals see the personal and organizational rewards for filling these vital linking roles (review Figure 9-2).

Core values and beliefs provide a foundation from which critical roles may evolve. Organizations with clear core values are much more likely to have the several types of roles evolve and act together. When core values are not clear or are inconsistent, they are associated with a chaotic informal organization and a stunted or conflictual set of critical roles. For example, in Laffer's organization, one reason that no key roles evolved to handle technology transfer was that technology transfer and interdivisional cooperation was not valued. At Harris Corporation, where technology transfer is a core value, there are numerous boundary spanners linking the divisions.

As with norms and climate, a clear set of core values can energize an organization in a focused direction. Inconsistency in core values will result in an unfocused and amorphous informal organization with diffuse norms and unconnected critical roles. Of the dimensions of organizational culture, then, core values assume particular importance. While norms, climate, and critical roles will evolve in their own idiosyncratic fashion in the absence of clear core values, they will evolve in a focused fashion in the context of clear and consistent core values (review Figure 9-3).

Core values, norms, climate, and key roles are important dimensions of organizational culture. Organizations are made up of multiple cultures. While some firms have a corporate culture (e.g., IBM, HP, DEC, Delta Airlines), even in these organizations there are substantial cultural differences within areas. For example, while Data General had developed an aggressive corporate culture (in part to distinguish itself from DEC), areas within Data General had very different cultures. Tom West created a culture of intensity, excellence, and an "us versus them" mentality, whereas other development areas at Data General had completely different norms and values. Similarly, production areas at GTE hold costs, volume, and efficiency as particularly vital, while R&D professionals are less committed to efficiency and much more committed to long-term research and complete understanding of a phenomenon.

Because different components of organizations have fundamentally different strategies and tasks, they need to develop unique cultures and informal organizations. Since these organizational groups are interdependent, they must also develop an informal organization to complement structural linking. The issue of managing culture, then, is one for all levels of the organization. Norms, values, and critical roles must be shaped to get the group's work as well as the organization's work done; that is, they must be shaped to deal with strategic linking.

## CULTURE AND PERFORMANCE

Culture is clearly an important aspect of organizations. Peters and Waterman found that corporate culture was an essential quality of excellent companies. A thread through the Japanese management literature is the importance of corporate culture. Excellent companies seem to have highly focused and widely shared values and work hard at keeping these values intact. For example, at IBM the trilogy of core values—service, human resources, and excellence—has remained stable since Thomas Watson, Sr., even though corporate strategies have dramatically changed. On the other hand, some organizations have highly focused values but are not excellent performers. For examples, U.S. Steel and Penn Central had unambiguous core values, yet both institutions suffered precisely *because* of these strongly held core values. Finally, organizations with unclear or inconsistent core values are consistently mediocre performers. For example, in Medtek's R&D facility, the absence of clear values from senior management resulted in an R&D facility's going off in several directions at once, adversely affecting innovation.

Culture is not directly associated with excellent performance. Focused culture seems to be a necessary but not sufficient condition for effective performance. Widely shared values and norms are associated with focused behavior. These focused behaviors may (e.g., IBM) or may not (e.g., U.S. Steel) be associated with effective performance. Companies with inconsistent values (e.g., Medtek or Federal Engineering) exhibit fragmented behaviors, which, in turn, are associated with less effective performance.

How does corporate culture affect behavior? In strongly focused cultures, because core values are pushed and evaluated constantly, employees down the line give extraordinary attention to those values. Given the passion for cleanliness at McDonalds, employees at every level go out of their way to keep their stations spotless. Similarly, managers can make marginally better decisions in the face of ambiguity if guided by a clear set of values and beliefs. For example, product and international business managers at Citibank are able to make coordinated decisions because they are embedded in a culture that emphasizes innovation and aggressiveness. On the other hand, given corporate confusion as to the value of international business at Corning Glass Works in the mid-1970s, the product and international business had enormous trouble in collaborating.

Finally, at the individual level, to the extent that one identifies with and internalizes the firm's core values, he or she will be intrinsically motivated to act in accord with those values. This personal identification with the organization's core values is an important source of energy and focused behavior in organizations and is associated with substantial social inertia—the propensity to hold on to and reinforce these core values and associated behaviors over time.

Strong cultures provide value anchors for individuals and groups. Clear and consistent cultures are associated with focused behaviors, which may or may not lead to effective performance. Conflicting or diffuse cultures lead to inconsistent and uncoordinated behaviors and lower performance. Strong cultures lead to both focused behaviors and built-in social inertia to reinforce those values and associated behaviors over time. Both Laffer and Shaeffer (review opening vignettes) face cultures that work against effective coordination between interdependent areas. Both the systems business at Federal Engineering and Laffer's technology transfer board require a shift in values and norms away from independence and conflictual relations toward values based on joint problem solving and corporate performance. Structural linking was not sufficient in bringing those interdependent units together. Both executives must complement their strategic linking choices with efforts to shape the different cultures.

More generally, core norms, values, and critical roles may help or hinder organizational coordination. Managers must develop appropriate cultures to deal effectively with work-related interdependence. The more complex the work-related interdependence, the more complex, rich, and diverse the culture must be to handle the increased problem-solving demands. For example, as long as Federal Engineering divisions were independent, norms regarding collaboration and joint problem solving were not important. However, as soon as interdependence increased (as it must in the systems business), the informal organization must develop norms, values, and key roles to handle the increased problem-solving demands within and between multiple levels of each division (review Figure 9-1).

As with structural linking mechanisms, the cultural intensity between groups must match the demands of work interdependence. When there is a mismatch between the nature of the information-processing requirements and the characteristics of the culture, coordination and control suffers. Managers must shape organizational cultures to complement structural linking mechanisms; both should fit the demands of the unit's work interdependence. When there are cultural impediments to linking, management must diagnose what norms and/or values help and hinder linking and what key roles are absent. This diagnosis should lead to programs to shape, develop, and change cultural shortcomings and bolster cultural strengths.

## SHAPING ORGANIZATIONAL CULTURES

Three types of factors shape organizational cultures: external, historical, and internal. Where external factors are essentially fixed, management can affect historical and internal factors in shaping organizational cultures (see Figure 9-4).

### External factors

**External** factors are those forces outside the organization that shape values and beliefs. The organization is embedded in a context of national, regional, and local cultures as well as industrial and professional cultures. In addition, other general environmental factors, such as regulation, technological changes, and competition, may shape the core values of the organization. For example, the cultural patterns of a large New York City medical center would be shaped by the culture of the city (including the neighborhood in which the hospital is located), the industrial culture (health care), the professional cultures (physicians, nurses, social workers, health care managers), and such other environmental factors as the role of third parties (insurers, medicare, medicaid). All of these

FIGURE 9-4    Factors Affecting Organizational Culture

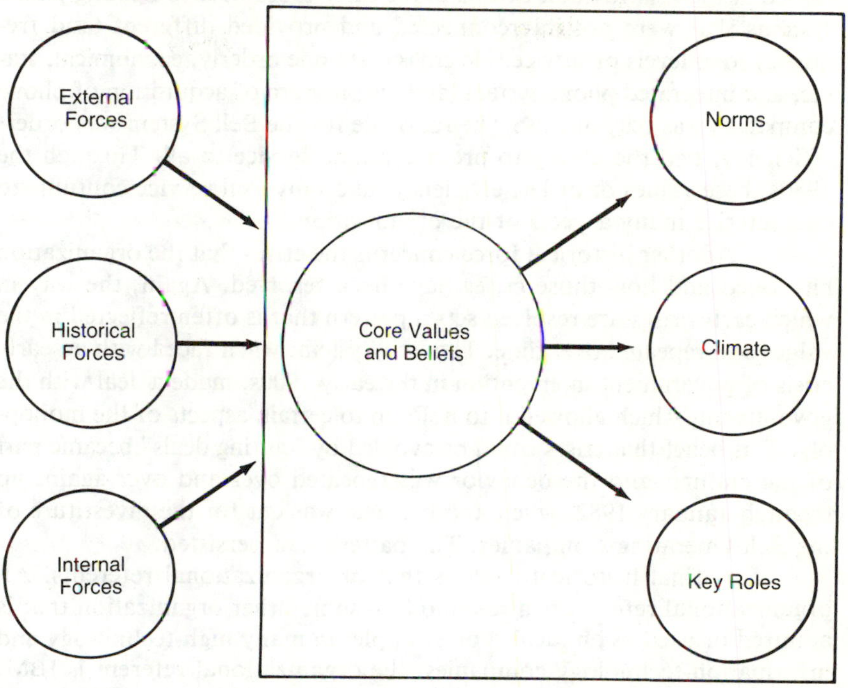

external forces have important effects on the values and beliefs that develop within the organization and within certain parts of the organization. These external factors are a constraint within which management must operate.

## Historical factors

**Organizational history** is also an important determinant of organizational culture. As with individuals, an organization's history (and in many cases, its early history in particular) has a very strong influence on the values and beliefs that develop over time. Several aspects of history are particularly important. One is the circumstances of the birth of the organization, or how the organization was founded. Important elements include how the founding came about, who the founders were, what the founders' values were, and what the emerging purpose or rationale of that organization was. Again, AT&T serves as a well-known example. The Bell System, as it was known through the early 1980s, was built largely through the efforts of one early executive, Theodore Vail. Vail was disturbed at the disarray that existed in the early 1900s with competing phone systems that were not interconnected and provided different (and frequency low) levels of service. He envisioned one orderly, economical, stable, and integrated phone system, and his program of acquisition of phone companies was part of that. The rationale for the Bell System was order, efficiency, and the ability to provide phone service to all. Through the 1980s these values of order, efficiency, and universal service continue to characterize many aspects of the organization.

Another historical force concerns the crises that the organization has faced and how those crises have been resolved. Again, the way in which early crises are resolved sets a pattern that is often reflected in the values and repeated over time. The Bell System, when faced with an early crisis of government intervention in the early 1900s, made a deal with the government, which allowed it to hold on to certain aspects of the monopoly. This belief that crises could be avoided by "cutting deals" became part of the culture, and the behavior was repeated over and over again, up through January 1982, when another deal was cut for the divestiture of the Bell Operating Companies. The pattern had persisted.

A final historical force is that of organizational referents. An organizational referent is a role model—some other organization that is admired or used as an ideal. For example, in many high-technology and information-technology companies, the organizational referent is IBM. People talk about how things are done at IBM and hold it up as the model for action. For many diversified companies, General Electric is the referent. In wholesale banking, Morgan Bank is seen as a model, while in quantitatively oriented business schools, the University of Chicago and Carnegie-Mellon University are frequent referents. In some cases, active efforts are made to recruit individuals from the referent companies. The referent is the expression of organizational aspirations—what it would like to be, what it wishes it could be, what it hopes to be. The implication is that "if we act like them, then we will be successful like them." Behavior is, in turn, shaped by this, sometimes in a thoughtful attempt to be like the referent, and at other times in surface-level mimicry.

## Internal factors

Finally, a host of **internal factors** shape organizational culture. Four elements are critical here: leadership behavior, strategic definition, structure, and human resource systems (see Figure 9-5). Perhaps the most critical shaper of organizational culture is the behavior of key leaders. Through their day-in/day-out behaviors, managers shape the social fabric of their organizations. In an inherently complex world, managers must make sense of organizational complexity and provide direction and energy

FIGURE 9-5     Key Internal Forces That Shape Culture

---

**Leadership Behavior**

| Articulation of Strategy | — How leaders verbalize the strategy |
| Modeling/Mundane Behavior | — How leaders provide visible models of desirable traits or behaviors |
| Personal Rewards | — How leaders use their personal behavior, recognition, or resources as rewards for behaviors that are consistent with the culture |
| Symbolic Behavior | — Specific behaviors (history, stories, heroes) that have symbolic value in sending messages about the culture |

**Strategic Definition**

| Role | — The current rationale: why the organization exists or how it defines its basic purpose |
| Choice of Businesses | — Types of activities the organization engages in |
| Competitive Basis | — How the organization defines the basis on which it will compete and its orientation toward competitors |
| Goals | — The nature of the targets that it sets for itself |
| Core Values | — The values that are explicit in the strategy |

**Structure**

| Organization Design | — Basic architecture of the organization: how units are formed, grouped, and linked |
| Rewards/Measure | — What behavior or activity is measured and what is rewarded; output and behaviors |
| Physical Arrangements | — Specific physical and locational aspects of the organization (layout, office design, physical symbols) |

**Human Resource Systems**

| Selection | — The type of people chosen to become part of the organization |
| Socialization | — How people brought into the organization are taught the core values and desired behavior |
| Staffing | — What kinds of people with what types of values, skills, and orientations get what jobs |
| Mobility | — How people move from job to job, function to function, or between parts of the organization |
| Human Resource Orientations | — The organization's commitment to the employees' welfare |

---

for their colleagues. In the context of clear, consistent messages, individuals get a sense of direction and value. Inconsistent and/or unbelievable messages add confusion and chaos to a system that only gets reduced by emergent informal dynamics. For example, the inconsistency of laboratory management at Medtek created confusion among personnel, which, in turn, was related to feelings of isolation and helplessness. Many of the sagas of successful organizational turnarounds, however, focus on how senior managers provide a tone, energy level, and direction for their firms (e.g., Wilson at Xerox; West at Data General; Watson at IBM; Ford at Ford; Sloan at GM).

Managers can shape culture and infuse their organizations with value in a variety of ways. The range of techniques involves sending a clear set of signals as to what kind of organization the manager wants, what key values he or she holds dear, and what kinds of behaviors are expected. For example, managers must articulate objectives and values for their organization. Without a clear sense of direction, the emergent organization will come up with its own set of objectives and values. The manager must provide a visible role model of the kinds of behaviors, norms, and values he or she demands. Here attention to mundane behavior is vital. What meetings are attended, what is first on the agenda versus what is last (and therefore not covered), and where managers spend their time and who they are seen with, are examples of small behaviors that send important information to subordinates and peers about what is held as important. Again, inconsistent messages create confusion and disorder about what managers stand for.

Personal rewards are also an important vehicle for shaping behaviors and values. Managers must use formal and informal rewards to reinforce behaviors that are consistent with their core values. Recognition, praise, attention, and perks, as well as formal rewards, must be clearly linked to behavior in support of core values. Managers can also shape core values and beliefs by telling stories and jokes, creating heroes, and interpreting history for their subordinates. Jokes, stories, and heroes are all mundane vehicles for shaping a vision or clarifying core values. For example, jokes at Citibank often have an aggressive and action orientation, reflecting Citibank's core values. Similarly, at AT&T, senior management must create new stories and heroes reflecting effective marketing and competition. At the same time, the older stories highlighting service at all costs are deemphasized.

Management can, then, shape core values and behavior through sustained personal attention to detail. While structure, strategy, and controls are important managerial levers, so too are mundane, day-to-day behaviors. Sustained attention to detail, focused communication through words, deeds, and symbols, can directly shape an organization's culture. Managers do not have to be charismatic. Rather, using everyday behavior clearly and consistently can directly shape organizational culture. However, if these mundane behaviors are inconsistent, if managers send out mixed messages, the informal organization will fill that value vacuum with its own values and associated culture.

Clarity of strategic definition is another factor that helps shape organizational cultures. The definition of the organization's purpose and how it will achieve that purpose are determinants of core values and norms. Definitions of products, markets, distinctive competence, and competitive timing are all important in shaping culture. An organization that consistently strives to be an industry leader with innovative, high-quality products and to stretch goals will develop a different culture than an organization that establishes a strategy of being a "me-too" competitor and low-cost producer. Similarly, at Federal Radar, the strategy of product leadership in distinct markets will encourage divisional based cultures, while the new systems strategy requires an overarching corporate culture based on synergy and collaboration.

Core values can be built into the organization's strategy. At IBM, ARCO, Tandem, and Delta, the organization's distinctive competence and core values are explicitly stated and managed. For example, ARCO's strategy includes statements about what the firm stands for: technical excellence, a people-orientation, and social responsibility. Similarly, there is no ambiguity about the core values in Peters and Waterman's excellent companies. Each firm's core values are an integral part of its strategy statement.

Organization structure also directly shapes organizational cultures. Strategic grouping focuses resources, shapes patterns of interaction, and conveys what is most strategically important. At Medtek, for example, the switch to a matrix structure in the laboratory sent a clear signal as to the importance of markets and technology. At 3M, a multitude of small divisions signals the importance of innovation, entrepreneurship, and flexibility.

Reward and control systems also convey important information about what is valued in an organization. Those organizations that espouse cooperation between departments but reward individual excellence send out mixed messages as to what is important. Reward systems must reflect organizational values. If cooperation, functional performance, and long- and short-run innovation is important, control systems must evaluate each of these seemingly inconsistent outputs. To reinforce their values of cooperation, Japanese organizations evaluate both outputs as well as attributes of behavior (how cooperative, helpful, and so on).

Physical location, size of offices, and location of resources also affect organizational culture. For example, those organizations in which managers have choice parking spaces, larger offices, and a separate dining room convey a different set of core values than do those organizations in which all are treated equally. The idea of branch laboratories at AT&T, in which branch laboratories of Bell Labs were placed next to Western Electric facilities, symbolized AT&T's commitment to link R&D with manufacturing. Similarly, moving Xerox' headquarters away from Rochester symbolized this firm's shift away from a single-product orientation to a more diversified, multinational corporation.

Human resource systems also directly affect organizational cultures. The types of individuals hired, the training and socialization of new recruits, and available career paths all directly shape organizational culture. Those organizations that hire young employees and promote from within, that engage in intense socialization and training, and that manage career paths so that individuals see different areas of the corporation will develop a focused organizational culture. Tom West at Data General created his own can-do, workaholic, aggressive, and independent culture by carefully selecting young engineers, giving them enormous responsibility early, having them "sign up" for intense schedules, and letting the informal organization socialize the recruits as to expected behaviors.

Japanese organizations pay special attention to human resource systems. They tend to hire young college graduates, engage in intensive socialization around the organization's core values, and develop an internal labor market in which individuals expect to become generalists (as opposed to functional specialists) and to move up the hierarchy in a lockstep fashion. While the content of Tom West's culture is dramatically different from typical Japanese culture, they both use human resource systems to shape those norms, values, and key roles.

The organization's human resource orientation also affects corporate culture. The organization's commitment to and concern for its employees as reflected in employee involvement programs, wholistic concern for the employee, long-term employment, and internal promotion patterns shape how individuals treat each other and what they expect from each other and the organization. For example, whereas some firms put a premium on human resources (e.g., IBM, DEC), others espouse the value of the free market and individual mobility (e.g., Data General in the early 1980s).

As we examine the set of factors that shape organization cultures, several implications emerge. First, some factors are beyond the control of management. In particular, some external forces may not be controllable. The external environment is usually the context within which managers work and which cannot be affected in the short run. Second, management has several key tools with which to shape culture. Management can affect organizational cultures through the internal leverage points of leadership behavior, strategy, structure, and human resource management systems. Another key tool is the ability to reshape or reinterpret organizational history. History can be actively shaped to enliven and give new meaning to organizational values, beliefs, and referents. Third, internal, and to some extent historical, forces are driven by management's behaviors and statements. Management must be sensitive to their personal role as vital shapers of organization culture.

Returning to Shaeffer and Laffer, both executives must work to shape the climate for collaboration and joint problem solving. In the short run, both managers must make it crystal clear that cooperation is vital to corporate, as well as to individual, performance. They must make clear, every day and in every way, the importance of these new values; they must demonstrate in their own behaviors the kind of behaviors they demand from their subordinates. Further, Shaeffer and Laffer need to promote and informally reward individuals who support the new organization designs. Shaeffer and Laffer can create champions and boundary spanners by differentially rewarding and encouraging, and being sponsors of, individuals who can push systems work at Federal Engineering and technology transfer at Office Products Company. In the longer term, if systems and technology transfer are to be important, then both organizations must develop structures, rewards, and human resource systems to enhance interdivisional coordination. Both managers must bolster the strategic linking choices with appropriate norms, values, and critical roles.

## ORGANIZATION CULTURE AS A DOUBLE-EDGED SWORD

Organizational culture has a profound effect on individual behavior. In well-developed cultures, focused behaviors are driven by an identification of the individual with his or her group and organization. Organizational culture takes on a life of its own as institutionalization processes carry core norms and values long after the initial charismatic leader is gone. Over time, local histories, heroes, and myths evolve that embody and perpetuate the organization's culture. While it takes time for these institutionalization processes to operate, once core norms and values are created, they carry enormous social inertia.

Organization culture is, then, a double-edged sword. Culture can be the cornerstone of the informal organization that influences behavior and performance in the desired direction. Clear, coherent, intense cultures can add enormous positive energy to an organization and can support the formal organization. In some cases, the informal organization actually replaces the formal system by doing some functions in a less costly and more effective manner. Ideally, culture is consistent with the organization's strategy, work, people, and formal organization.

On the other hand, organization cultures can become obsolete. If strategy changes or if the nature of the work changes (as they did at Federal Engineering, for example), previously functional cultures may become profoundly dysfunctional. Unlike strategy, tasks, or structures, which can be changed rapidly, organization culture is extremely difficult to change. Given individual commitment and organizational institution-alization processes, culture persists and acts as a social anchor. While strategy, structure, and individuals may change, culture frequently remains rooted in the organization's past and sows the seeds of conflict and trauma.

These traumas are accentuated when previously functional cultures, in which people were proud and heavily invested, are suddenly rendered inconsistent by sudden changes in strategy, objectives, and/or technologies. For example, at AT&T, the Ma Bell culture has been built and reinforced for over sixty years. This culture, rooted in service, standardization, and engineering dominance, helped create the world's finest telephone system. However, it is precisely the Ma Bell mentality that hinders the new AT&T from effectively competing in the office products and computer markets. Similarly, it is Federal Engineering's success that is at the root of its interdivisional conflicts as it attempts to jump into the systems business.

Organization cultures must change as strategies and/or objectives change. The challenge in managing cultural change is to reinforce as many of the core values as possible, to bolster links to the past even while pruning obsolete values and adding core values that reflect current strategic contingencies. The notion of pruning core values is a helpful image in that managers want to retain as much of this historically rooted energy as possible, yet redirect it in line with current competitive realities. Xerox, for example, is attempting to hold tight to the firm's core values of customer satisfaction, innovation, and commitment to human resources, and to bolster these with the notion of leadership through quality. Apple Computer is attempting to retain its emphasis on technological excellence, even as it adds a new focus on marketing and customer service. In this way, both Xerox and Apple employees can hold on to a proud history and step out to meet current challenges.

## SUMMARY

### Opening cases revisited:

All three of the general managers pictured in the opening cases — Shaeffer, Laffer, and Roberts — face significant challenges for which there are no easy answers. Each of them face the fact that their organization design efforts, while necessary, are not sufficient for bringing about the type of change and reorientation that each feels is required for his or her particular situation. In each case, the general manager will need to examine the organizational culture and understand to what extent that culture fits with or supports the structural work that has been done. To the extent that there is poor fit between the culture and the other elements (such as organization design and strategy), each manager needs to consider the possible types of cultural changes and how he or she can use the leverage points available to start to initiate the required changes.

Core values, norms, organization climate, and critical roles have a profound effect on behavior in organizations. Strong, clear cultures focus behavior, which is, in turn, associated with either functional or dysfunctional consequences. If management does not shape organizational culture, it will evolve on its own, driven by local interests within the organization. Levers to shape culture include strategy, structure, human resource systems, and, most importantly, direct managerial behavior.

While culture is a generically important organizational issue, it has particular import in strategic linking. Management must develop norms, values, and key roles to complement structural linking in the service of enhanced coordination between interdependent units. Both structure and informal processes are required to achieve effective linking. The more complex the work-related interdependence, the more rich and complex must be the structural linking mechanisms and the organization culture in order to handle the substantial problem-solving requirements. To the extent that the culture is inconsistent with linking requirements, management must deal with the difficulties of shaping culture in the face of socially anchored inertia.

## NOTES

1. This chapter builds on an extensive literature on organization culture, climate, and informal dynamics, including S. Davis, *Managing Corporate Culture*, (Cambridge, MA: Ballinger, 1984); N. Hatvany and V. Pucik, "An Integrated Management System Focused on Human Resources: The Japanese Paradigm," in D. Nadler, M. Tushman, and N. Hatvany, *Managing Organizations*, (Boston, MA: Little, Brown, 1982); R. Kilman, M. Saxton, and R. Serpa, *Gaining Control of the Corporate Culture*, (San Francisco, CA: Jossey-Bass, 1985); G. Litwin and R. Stringer, *Motivation and Organizational Climate*, (Boston, MA: Harvard Graduate School of Business, 1968); M. Louis, "Organizations as

Culture-Bearing Milieux," in L. R. Pondy, ed., *Organizational Symbolism*, (Greenwich, CT: JAI Press, 1983); W. Ouchi, *Theory Z*, (Reading, MA: Addison-Wesley, 1981); T. Peters and R. Waterman, *In Search of Excellence*, (New York: Harper & Row, 1982); J. Pfeffer, *Power in Organizations*, (Marshfield, MA: Pitman, 1981); E. Schein, *Organizational Culture and Leadership*, (San Francisco, CA: Jossey-Bass, 1985).

2. For an in-depth view of Data General's informal organization, see T. Kidder, *Soul of a New Machine*, (Boston, MA: Little, Brown, 1982).

3. E. Roberts and A. Fusfeld, "Critical Functions: Needed Roles in the Innovation Process," in R. Katz, ed., *Career Issues in Human Resource Management*, (Englewood Cliffs, NJ: Prentice-Hall, 1982); M. Tushman, "Managing Communication Networks in R&D Laboratories," *Sloan Management Review* 20 (1979): 37–49.

# 10

# Implementing New Designs: Managing Organizational Change

**Case:**

Orient Oil Corporation is a major force in the energy industry. About ten years ago, Orient senior management decided to diversify out of petroleum-based industries into other ventures, some related to the basic business and some completely unrelated. For a while, this seemed to work out. After the first three years of the acquisition strategy, Orient faced problems in managing the different companies within its structure, so it called in a consulting firm, which did an organization study and recommended the establishment of twenty-three individual strategic business units, each with its own president and a complete set of staff functions. The business units were in turn grouped into four major sectors, each headed by a senior corporate executive.

About four years into the strategy, things started to go sour. Many of the management systems, approaches, and methods that had worked so well in the oil business seemed to lead to one disaster after another. For a while, the huge profits of the oil business could be used to cover up the continuing stream of catastrophes in the other units, but finally it became obvious to both insiders and outsiders that Orient was incapable of effectively managing businesses outside its basic industry. A strategic decision was made to start divesting or liquidating the acquisitions and to move back to the base business.

A very senior group was convened to work intensively for

several weeks to develop a plan to reorganize the company. They produced a top secret document that proposed reorganizing the company into two major operating units — one focusing primarily on energy exploration and production and the other focusing on refining, distribution, and sales. A third group would hold the non-energy-related business but would be chartered to do itself out of business in two years through divestiture or liquidation.

The policy committee of the corporation met for a full-day session to hear the report of the design task force and, after many hours of debate, decided to go ahead with the group's recommendations. Having worked hard for several hours, the group took a short break at about 4:00 in the afternoon and decided to reconvene at 4:30 to "tie up the loose ends."

As the meeting started again, the discussion moved toward the issue of announcements. Many members of the group were pushing for an immediate announcement. Rumors were flying around the company that something was up, and the group members were concerned about the consequences of possible information leaks. In the midst of this discussion, one of the group turned to the task force chairman and said, "Once we make the announcement, what do you want people to do then?" The task force chairman looked around the room for help and saw none. He responded, "Well, there's a lot we haven't figured out yet. We'll just tell people not to worry about it." The questioner came back, "Aren't we just creating problems, then, by announcing this thing? We're just going to disturb people, and nobody will be doing any work." The room was silent.

## INTRODUCTION

As with Orient Oil, many managers see their organization design work as completed when "the announcement" is made. Because so much energy may have been expended on reaching an agreement on a design, little thought may have been given to what will happen next. As a result, after the announcement is made, managers suddenly begin to think about how to manage the implementation of the change in design.

In fact, implementing a new design is difficult, as is the implementation of any major change within an organization. Design changes are particularly problematic because it seems so easy to create a design on paper that managers often overlook how truly difficult it is to install a new design and make it work effectively. Truly effective implementation is difficult and often takes a good deal of time.

Many design failures—in which everyone agrees that the reorganization was a disaster—are not failures because of a technically inadequate design but rather are failures of implementation. In practice, an adequate or even mediocre design, if implemented well, can be effective, while the most elegant and sophisticated of designs poorly implemented will fail.

This chapter, then, will be devoted to the question of implementation of organization designs. The underlying issue in design implementation appears to be one of managing organizational change. We will therefore start by providing a way of thinking about changes in organization. Next, we will point out some of the very predictable problems that one encounters when attempting to bring about change. Finally, we will discuss some implications for managing change and outline some specific techniques and action areas for enhancing the implementation of organization design changes.

## CRITERIA FOR ORGANIZATIONAL CHANGE

During the past decade, there has been increasing interest in the subject of managing organizational change.[1] One approach to thinking about change that many have found useful was originally proposed by Richard Beckhard and Reuben Harris. They saw the implementation of a change, such as a new organization design, as the moving of an organization toward a desired future state. They saw changes in terms of transitions (see Figure 10-1). At any time, an organization exists in a **current state (A)**. The current state describes how the organization functions prior to a change. In terms of our congruence model, we can think of the current state as a particular configuration of the strategy, task, individual, and formal and informal organizations. A change involves movement

FIGURE 10-1    Organization Change as Transition

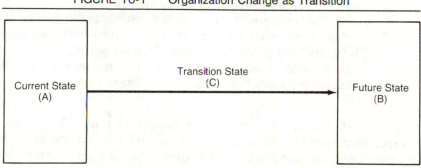

toward a desired **future state** (B), which describes how the organization should function after the change. In a design, the full set of design documents (strategic design, impact analysis, operational design, and so on) provides a written description of the intended future state.

The period between the current state (A) and the future state (B) can be thought of as the **transition state** (C). In the most general terms, then, the effective management of change involves developing an understanding of the current state, developing an image of the desired future state, and moving the organization through a transition period. In design, we deal with the first two of these steps. Implementation concerns the moving of the organization through the transition period. Typically, as much care needs to be taken in designing the transition as in designing the future state—both are critical.

Several criteria can be used to judge the effective management of transitions. Building on the transition framework just presented, an organizational change, such as the implementation of a new design, can be managed effectively when:

1. The organization is moved from the current state to the future state—in which the design is actually installed or implemented.

2. The functioning of the organization design in the future state meets expectations, or works as planned. In the case of design, this means that the design in practice met the criteria that it was intended to satisfy.

3. The transition is accomplished without undue cost to the organization. This means that the design is implemented without significant disruptions to the business or damage to relationships with customers, suppliers, or regulators. While there is always some cost associated with implementation, the cost should be managed, predictable, and controlled consistent with the estimates done in the impact analysis. "Undue" cost is cost that is unplanned, unpredicted, or uncontrolled.

4. The transition is accomplished without undue cost to individual organization members. Here again, the key operative word is "undue" as defined by the original impact analysis. Much of the cost to individuals occurs more through the manner in which changes are made than through the change itself.

Of course, not every implementation of a new design can be expected to meet all of these criteria consistently, but such standards provide a target for planning implementation. The question is how to maximize the chances that the design will be implemented effectively.

# PROBLEMS OF IMPLEMENTING ORGANIZATIONAL CHANGES

What are the issues that must be addressed if managers are to implement effectively? On the broadest level, there are two basic issues — what the change should be and how the change should be implemented. Throughout this book we have been dealing with the first issue as it relates to organization design. We have stressed the importance of diagnosis of problems and causes, followed by systematic work to develop and then choose from alternative solutions that will be responsive to those problems. The second question — how the changes are implemented — is the one on which we will focus now. Observations of changes seem to indicate that there are three types of problems encountered in some form whenever a significant organizational change is attempted.

## The problem of power

Any organization is a political system made up of various individuals, groups, and coalitions competing for power. Political behavior is thus a natural and expected feature of organizations. Such behavior occurs during the current and future states. In the transition state, however, these dynamics become even more intense as an old design, with its political implications, is dismantled and a new design takes its place. Any significant change (and design changes clearly are significant in terms of power) poses the possibility of upsetting or modifying the balance of power among various formal and informal interest groups. The uncertainty created by change creates ambiguity, which in turn tends to increase the probability of political activity as people try to create some structure and certainty by attempting to control their environment.

Individuals and groups may take political action based on their perceptions of how the change will affect their relative power position in the organization. They will try to influence where they will sit in the organization (both formal and informal) that emerges from the transition and will be concerned about how the conflict of the transition period will affect the balance of power in the future state. Finally, individuals and groups may engage in political action because of their ideological position with regard to the change — the new design, strategy, or approach may be inconsistent with their shared values or their image of the organization.

## The problem of anxiety

Change in organizations involves the movement from something that is known toward something that is unknown. Individuals naturally have concerns, such as whether they will be needed in the new organization, whether their skills will be valued, and how they will cope with the new situation. These concerns can be summarized in the question that is frequently voiced during a major organizational change—"what's going to happen to me?" To the extent that this question cannot fully be answered (such as in the Orient Oil case at the beginning of this chapter), individuals may experience stress and feel anxious.

As stress and anxiety increase, they may result in a variety of behavior or performance problems. For example, stress may result in difficulty in hearing or integrating information. It may lead people to resist changes that they might otherwise support or in the extreme, engage in irrational and even self-destructive acts. Resistance is a common occurrence, although in many large organizations people may not actively resist the change by openly refusing to implement the new organization design. What does occur is that people passively or subtly resist the change or act in ways that objectively do not appear to be constructive for either the individual or the organization.

## The problem of organizational control

A significant change in organization design tends to disrupt the normal course of events within the organization. Thus, it frequently undermines existing systems of management control, particularly those that are embedded in the formal organizational arrangements. An impending change may suddenly make control systems irrelevant or cause them to be perceived as "lame ducks." As a result, it is often easy to lose control during a change. As goals, structures, and people shift, it becomes difficult to monitor performance and make correct assumptions, as one would during a more stable period.

A related problem is that most of the formal organizational arrangements are designed either to manage the current state (the existing design) or to manage the future state (the proposed new design), but those same designs may not be adequate for the management of the transition state. In most situations, they are not appropriate for managing implementation, since they are steady state management systems designed to run organizations already in place. They are not transitional management devices.

## IMPLICATIONS FOR CHANGE MANAGEMENT

Each of these three problems leads to some relatively straightforward conclusions about actions needed to manage change (see Fig-

FIGURE 10-2     Change Problems and Implications

| Problem | Implication |
| --- | --- |
| Power ⟶ | Need to shape the political dynamics associated with change |
| Anxiety ⟶ | Need to motivate constructive behavior in response to the change |
| Control ⟶ | Need to systematically manage the transition state |

ure 10-2). To the extent that a change presents the possibility of significant power problems, the management of the organization's political system must shape the political dynamics associated with the change, preferably prior to implementation. Second, to the extent that change creates anxiety and the associated patterns of dysfunctional behavior, it is critical to motivate individuals, through communications and rewards, to react constructively to the change. Finally, if a change presents significant control problems, this implication is the need to pay attention to the management of the transition state to ensure effective organizational control during the transition period. The question is how to do this. There appear to be some patterns in the effectively managed changes. While not universal principles, they represent some relatively consistent differences between the actions that managers take in effective cases of change management and the actions taken in ineffective cases.

For each of the three implications for change management, there are four actions that appear to characterize effectively managed changes. On the following pages, each action area will be explained and a list of illustrative techniques associated with each area will be discussed. The summaries of these techniques are listed in Figures 10-3, 10-4, and 10-5, respectively.

## Action areas for shaping political dynamics

The first set of practices concerns the organization as a political system. Any significant change usually involves some modification of the political system, thus raising issues of power. The implication is a need to shape and manage the political dynamics prior to and throughout the transition. This concept relates to four specific action areas.

The first action area involves getting the support of key power groups within the organization in order to build a critical mass in favor of the change. The organization is a political system with competing groups, cliques, coalitions, and interests, each with varying views on any

FIGURE 10-3     Shaping Political Dynamics

| Action | Purpose | Technique |
|---|---|---|
| Get support of key power groups | Build internal critical mass of support for change | Identify power relationships<br>— Key players<br>— Stakeholders<br>— Influence relationships<br>Use strategies for building support<br>— Participation<br>— Bargaining/deals<br>— Isolation<br>— Removal |
| Demonstrate leadership support of the change | Shape the power distribution and influence the patterns of behavior | Leaders model behavior to promote identification with them<br>Articulate vision of future state<br>Use reward system<br>Provide support/resources<br>Remove roadblocks<br>Maintain momentum<br>Send signals through informal organization |
| Use symbols | Create identification with the change and appearance of a critical mass of support | Communicate with:<br>— Names/graphics<br>— Language systems<br>— Symbolic acts<br>— Small signals |
| Build in stability | Reduce excess anxiety, defensive reactions, and conflicts | Allow time to prepare for change<br>Send consistent messages<br>Maintain points of stability<br>Communicate what will not change |

particular change. Some favor the change. Some oppose it. Some may be disinterested. But the change cannot succeed unless there is a critical mass of support; several steps can be used to build that support. The first step is identifying the power relationships as a basis for planning a political strategy. This step may involve identifying the key players in the organization, or the individual and/or group stakeholders—the individuals who have a positive, negative, or neutral stake in the change. Frequently, drawing a diagram or creating a stakeholder or influence map may be useful in conceptualizing these relationships. This map should include not only the various stakeholders but their relationships to each other—who influences whom and what the stakes are for each individual.

Having identified the political topography of the change, the next step is to think about approaches for building support. There are several possible methods. The first is participation, which has long been recognized as a tool for reducing resistance to change and for gaining support. As individuals or groups become involved in a change, they tend to see it as *their* change, rather than one imposed on them.

Participation, while desirable, might not be feasible or wise in all situations. In some cases, participation merely increases the power of opposing groups to forestall the change. Thus, another approach may be bargaining with groups, or cutting deals. In this case, those favoring the change get the support of others by providing some incentive to comply.

A third step is isolation. There may be those who resist participation or bargaining and who persist in attempting to undermine the change. The goal in this situation is to minimize the impact of such individuals on the organization by assigning them to a position outside the mainstream.

In the extreme, the final step is removal. In some cases, individuals who cannot be isolated or brought into constructive roles may have to be removed from the scene through a transfer to another organization or by outplacement. Obviously, participation and bargaining are more desirable and leave a more positive aftermath; however, it would be naive to assume that these first two methods will be successful in all cases.

An important consideration in creating the political momentum and sense of critical mass is the activity of leaders. Thus, a second action area is leader behavior in support of the change. Leaders can greatly shape the power distribution and influence patterns in an organization. They can mold perceptions and create a sense of political momentum by sending out signals, providing support, and dispensing rewards.

Leaders can take a number of specific actions. First, they can serve as models; through their behavior, they provide a vision of the future state and a source of identification for various groups within the organization. Second, leaders can serve as important persons in articulating the vision of the future state. Third, leaders can play a crucial role by rewarding key individuals and specific types of behavior. Fourth, leaders can provide support through political influence and needed resources. Similarly, leaders can remove roadblocks and, through their public statements, maintain momentum. Finally, leaders can send important signals through the informal organization. During times of uncertainty and change, individuals throughout the organization tend to look to leaders for signals concerning appropriate behavior and the direction of movement in the organization. Frequently, potent signals are sent through such minor acts as patterns of attendance at meetings or the phrases and words used in public statements. By careful attention to these subtle actions, leaders can greatly influence the perceptions of others.

The third action area concerns the use of symbols associated with a change. Such symbols as language, pictures, and acts create a focus for identification and the appearance of a critical mass within the organization's political system. Symbols are used by public and social movements and are similarly relevant to dealing with the political system within an organization. A variety of devices can be used, such as names and related graphics that clearly identify events, activities, or organizational units. Language is another symbol; it can communicate a unique way of doing business. The use of symbols is a mundane behavior that can, however, have a powerful impact on the clarity of the informal organization. The more focused the informal organization, the less the political turbulence. For example, a particular promotion, a firing, the moving of an office, or an open door, all can serve to create and send important signals. These small but visible signals by the leaders (as mentioned above) can be important in providing a symbolic sense of political movement.

The final action area is that of building stability. Too much uncertainty can create excess anxiety and defensive reaction, thus heightening political conflict to a counterproductive level. The organization must provide certain "anchors" to create a sense of stability within the context of the transition. This can help limit the reverberations of the change and dampen counterproductive political activity. A number of steps, such as preparing people for the change by providing information in advance, can buffer them to a degree against the uncertainty that will occur. Secondly, some stability can be preserved—even in the face of change—if managers are careful to maintain the consistency of messages they convey to organization members throughout the period of change. Nothing creates more instability than inconsistent or conflicting messages. Thirdly, it may be important to maintain certain very visible aspects of the business, such as preserving certain units, organizational names, management processes, or staffing patterns or keeping people in the same physical location. Finally, it may help to communicate specifically what will not change—to mediate the fears that everything is changing or that the change will be much greater than what actually is planned.

In summary, the four action areas focus on identifying the political system and then developing a political strategy. Specific action includes using leadership and related symbols to maintain momentum and critical mass in support of the change and building stability to prevent the counterproductive effects of extreme anxiety.

## Motivating constructive behavior

When a broad, significant change occurs in an organization, the first questions many people ask are "What's in it for me?" and "What's going to happen to me?" This is an indication of the anxiety that occurs when people are faced with the uncertainty associated with organizational change. Anxiety may result in a number of reactions, ranging from withdrawal to panic to active resistance. The task of management is to somehow relieve that anxiety and motivate constructive behavior through a variety of actions. Some actions are aimed at providing much needed information communicating the nature, extent, and impact of the change. Others are focused on providing clear rewards for required behavior, recognizing and dealing with some of the natural anxiety. There are four specific action areas.

FIGURE 10-4    Motivating Constructive Behavior

| Action | Purpose | Technique |
|---|---|---|
| Surface/create dissatisfaction with the current state | Unfreeze from the present state and provide motivation to move away from the present situation | Present information on:<br>— Environmental impact<br>— Economic impact<br>— Goal discrepancies<br>— How change affects people<br>Have organization members collect/present information |
| Obtain the appropriate levels of participation in planning/implementing change | Obtain the benefits of participation (motivation, better decisions, communication); control the costs of participation (time, control, conflict, ambiguity) | Create opportunities for participation<br>— Diagnosis<br>— Design<br>— Implementation planning<br>— Implementation evaluation<br>Use a variety of participation methods<br>— Direct/indirect<br>— Information vs. input vs. decision making<br>— Broad vs. narrow scope<br>— Expertise vs. representation |
| Reward desired behavior in transition to future state | Shape behavior to support the future state | Give formal rewards<br>— Measures<br>— Pay<br>— Promotion<br>Give informal rewards<br>— Recognition/praise<br>— Feedback<br>— Assignments |
| Provide time and opportunity to disengage from current state | Help people deal with their attachment and loss associated with change | Allow enough time<br>Create opportunity to vent emotions<br>Have farewell ceremonies |

The first action area is to surface or create dissatisfaction with the current state. Individuals may be psychologically attached to the current state, which is comfortable and known, compared to the uncertainty associated with change. A critical step, then, is to demonstrate how unrealistic it is to assume that the current state has been completely good, is still good, and will always remain good. The goal is to "unfreeze" people from their inertia and create willingness to explore the possibility of change. Part of their anxiety is based on fantasies that the future state may create problems, as well as on fantasies about how wonderful the current state is.

Techniques for dealing with this problem involve providing specific information, such as educating people about what is occurring in the environment that is creating the need for change. In addition, it is useful to help people understand the economic and business consequences of not changing. It may be helpful to identify and emphasize discrepancies — the discrepancy between the present situation and the situation as it should be. In critical cases, it may be necessary to paint a disaster scenario, in which people can see what would happen if the current state continued unchanged. It may be helpful to present a graphic image of how the failure to change would affect people. One manager for example, talked very graphically about what would happen if the division did not become successful within eighteen months: "They'll pull buses up to the door, close the plant, and cart away the workers and the machinery." The manager presented a highly graphic image of the consequences of not making the change. An alternative to management's presenting this kind of information may be to involve organization members in collecting and presenting their own perceptions. Participating in the collection and discovery process may make the information more salient, since it comes from peers in the work force.

There is a need to overcommunicate during change management efforts. Extreme anxiety impairs normal functioning; thus, people may be unable to hear and integrate messages effectively the first time. Therefore, it may be necessary to communicate key messages two, three, four, and even five times to individuals through various media.

The second action area for motivation is to obtain participation in planning and implementing change. Employee participation in the change process yields proven benefits. It tends to capture people's excitement. It may result in better decisions because of employee input, and it may create more direct communications through personal involvement. On the other hand, participation also has some cost. It takes time, involves giving up some control, and may create conflict and increase ambiguity. The question, then, is to choose where, how, and when to build in participation. People may participate in the early diagnosis of problems, in the design or development of solutions, in implementation planning, or in the actual execution of the implementation. There are many options. Various individuals or groups may participate at different times, depending on their skills and expertise, the information they have, and their acceptance and ownership of the change. Participation can be direct and widespread or indirect through representatives. Representatives may be chosen by position, level, or expertise. Using some form of participation usually outweighs the costs of no involvement at all.

The third action area is to visibly reward the desired behavior in both the future and transition states. People tend to do what they perceive they will be rewarded for doing. To the extent that people see their behavior as leading to rewards or outcomes they value, they will tend to be motivated to perform as expected. It is important to realize that during implementation, the old reward system frequently loses potency and new rewards are not set up as an early step. This results in a situation in which an individual is asked to act in one way but has been rewarded for acting in another way. Sometimes people are punished by the existing measurement system for doing things that are required to make the change successful. Management needs to pay special attention to the indicators of performance, to the dispensation of pay or other tangible rewards, and to promotion during the transition. In addition, there are informal rewards, such as recognition, praise, feedback, or the assignment of different roles, and it is important to carefully manage these to ensure that they support constructive behavior during the transition. It is equally important to reestablish clearly an appropriate reward system for the future state.

The fourth action area directly affects individual anxiety. It is the need to provide time and opportunity to disengage from the current state. People associate a sense of loss with change. It is predictable that they will go through a process of "letting go of," or mourning, the old structure. Management, knowing that this is essential, can greatly assist in this process. A number of specific techniques are possible. One is to provide the appropriate time for letting go, while giving people enough information and preparation to work through their detachment from the current state. Another technique may be to provide the opportunity to vent emotions through an event similar to a wake. This can be done in small group discussions, in which people are encouraged to talk about their feelings concerning the organizational change. While this may initially be seen as promoting resistance, it can have the opposite effect. People will undoubtedly talk about these issues, either formally or informally. If management can recognize such concerns and encourage people to express their feelings, it may help them let go of them and move into constructive action. It may also be useful to create ceremony, ritual, or symbols, such as fare-well or closing-day ceremonies, to help give people some psychological clo-sure on the old organization.

Thus, there are four action areas in motivating constructive behavior. One concerns helping people detach themselves from the cur-rent state. The second concerns obtaining appropriate levels of participa-tion in planning or implementing the change. The third concerns rewarding desired behavior during the transition, and the final action area has to do with helping people let go of their psychological attachment to the present situation.

## Managing the transition

The third implication concerns the actual and explicit manage-ment of the transition state, which is that time period between the current state and the implemented future state. It is frequently characterized by great uncertainty and control problems, because the current state is dis-assembled prior to full operation of the future state. Managers need to coordinate the transition with the same degree of care, the same resources, and the same skills as they manage any other major project. There are four specific action areas in which managers can work (see Figure 10-5).

The first action area is to develop and communicate a clear image of the future state. The ambiguity of change without a focus produces major problems. It is difficult to manage toward something when people do not know what that something is. In the absence of a clear direction, the organization gets "transition paralysis," and activity grinds to a halt. This is caused by uncertainty over what is appropriate, helpful, or con-structive behavior. Several specific practices are relevant in this situation. First, there is a need to develop as complete a design as possible for the future state. This may not always be feasible, but to the extent possible, it is important to articulate at least a vision ahead of time. Secondly, it may be useful to construct a statement that identifies the impact of the change on different parts of the organization. Thirdly, it is important to maintain a stable vision and to avoid unnecessary changes, extreme mod-ification, or conflicting views of that vision during the transition.

Finally, there is a need to communicate. As previously indicated, it is important to communicate repeatedly and to use multiple media, be it video, small group discussions, large group meetings, or written memos. It is critical to think of this communication as both a telling and a sell-

FIGURE 10-5    Managing the Transition

| Action | Purpose | Technique |
|---|---|---|
| Develop and communicate a clear image of the future state | Provide direction for management of transition; reduce ambiguity | Develop as complete a design as possible<br>Generate impact statements<br>Communicate<br>— Repeatedly<br>— Multiple channels<br>— Tell and sell<br>Describe how things will operate<br>Communicate clear, stable image/vision of the future |
| Use multiple and consistent leverage points | Recognize the systemic nature of changes and reduce potential for creating new problems during transition | Use all four organizational components<br>Anticipate poor fits<br>Sequence changes appropriately |
| Use transition devices | Create organizational arrangements specifically to manage the transition state | Appoint a transition manager<br>Provide transition resources<br>Design specific transition devices (dual systems, backup)<br>Develop a transition plan |
| Obtain feedback about the transition state; evaluate success | Determine the progress of the transition; reduce dependence on traditional feedback processes | Use formal methods<br>— Interviews<br>— Focus groups<br>— Surveys/samples<br>Use informal channels<br>Use participation |

ing activity. People need to be informed, but they also need to be sold on why the change is important. This may necessitate repeated explanations of the rationale for the change, the nature of the future state, and the advantages of the future. Finally, the future state must be made real, visible, and concrete. Communications should include information on future decision-making and operating procedures. The way in which this is communicated can help shape the vision of the future. For example, one company showed television commercials, both inside and outside its organization, demonstrating the specific types of customer service that it was attempting to provide. The commercials gave people clear, graphic, and memorable images of the future state.

The next area is to use multiple and consistent leverage points for changing behavior. This issue relates to the organizational model underlying this approach to change management. An organization is a system made of tasks, individuals, formal organizational arrangements, and informal organizational arrangements. During a transition, when certain aspects of the organization are being changed, there is a potential for problems arising from a poor fit. An organization works best when all elements fit smoothly. Managers need to use all of these levers for change. Specifically, managers need to think about modifications that need to be made in the work, individuals, formal structure, and informal arrangements. Secondly, there is a need to monitor and/or predict some of the poor fits that may occur when changing any of the organizational components. It is necessary to plan the changes to minimize poor fit among different elements of the organization.

The next action area involves using transition devices. The transition state is different from the current and future states; therefore, there may be a need to create organizational arrangements that are specifically designed to manage the transition state. These devices include: (1) a transition manager; (2) specific transition resources, including budget, time, and staff; (3) specific transition structures, such as dual management systems and backup support; and (4) a transition plan. All of these can be helpful in bringing needed management attention to the transition.

The final area is to obtain feedback and an evaluation of the transition state. The transition is a time when managers need to know what is going on in the organization. There is usually a breakdown in the normal feedback devices that managers use to collect information about how the organization is running. This is particularly serious during a period of change when there may be high anxiety and people hesitate to deliver bad news. Therefore, it is critical to build in various channels for feedback. Formal methods may include individual interviews, various types of focus-group data collection, surveys used globally or with select samples, or feedback gathered during a normal business meeting. Informal channels include senior managers's meeting with individuals or with groups, informal contacts, or field trips. Finally, feedback may be promoted through direct participation by representatives of key groups in planning, monitoring, or implementing the change.

In summary, the initial emphasis in transition management is on identifying a clear image of the future state. Secondly, there is a need to pay attention to the changing configuration of the organizational system and to develop—where needed—unique organizational arrangements to manage the transition period. Finally, there is a need to monitor progress through the development of feedback systems. All of these are important elements in managing a transition.

# SUMMARY

**Opening case revisited:**

The reorganization at Orient Oil presents the potential for a full range of problems associated with change. This change requires concentrated attention from skilled managers. In Orient, the senior team was exposed to a speaker who raised some of the key issues in managing change and described some new and different methods of change management. As a consequence, the senior group at Orient decided to delay the announcement of the change and appointed a highly respected senior member to head a transition team. This team was dedicated full time to the transition management task. The first assignment was to develop an initial transition plan, which included specific sections dealing with communications; how to get participation in the change; how to sequence the individual changes; how to assign jobs and coordinate moves; how to make the changes in information and control systems; and, finally, what the senior team had to do to lead the change effectively. The senior team reviewed this plan several weeks later and approved it. The change was implemented, led by the senior team, and guided by the transition manager and the transition team. Within six months, all of the major elements of the transition plan had been accomplished. As the Orient Oil chairman reflected, "When I think about all of the things we changed and all of the things we had to accomplish, I never thought that we could have done this so well. I'm amazed."

Why have we placed such an emphasis on change management? The process of implementation is a critical determinant of the success of a new organization design. To develop a design and then not give significant thought, time, and effort to the planning and management of its implementation is to do only part of the job of design.

As we look at organizations over time, we find that changes in design are a normal part of life. They are not one-time events but an ongoing element in the development of an organization. Adaptive organizations are able to respond quickly and effectively to new conditions—they are able to reconfigure to support new strategies as needed. Therefore, organizations that remain effective over time have to develop the capacity to execute change and, in some cases, competently manage accelerated change.

This leads us to our final topic: organizations over time. What are the types of design changes that we might anticipate at different points in time? Moreover, how might managers think ahead and begin to plan necessary changes in organization design in a way that anticipates rather than responds to problems and opportunities? Can creative organization design done in anticipation be an effective competitive tool for the manager?

## NOTES

1. R. Beckhard and R. Harris, *Organizational Transitions*, (Reading, MA: Addison-Wesley, 1977); M. Beer, *Organization Change and Development*, (Santa Monica, CA: Goodyear, 1980); N. Margulies and J. Wallace, *Organizational Change*, (Glenview, IL: Scott, Foresman, 1973); D. Nadler, *Feedback and Organization Development*, (Reading, MA: Addison-Wesley, 1977); N. Tichy, *Managing Strategic Change*, (New York: Wiley, 1983); M. Tushman, *Organization Change: An Exploratory Study and Case History*, (Ithaca, NY: NYSSILR, Cornell University, 1974).

# 11

# Designing Organizations: Organizational Evolution

The case studies that have introduced each chapter of this text describe organizations in some degree of crisis. Each involves problems of turnover and dissatisfaction of key individuals, conflict and lack of teamwork between groups, low quality innovation, poor service delivery, and/or difficulty in meeting challenging objectives. It is paradoxical that most of these vignettes take place in organizations, divisions, or functional groups that historically have been enormously successful. For example:

—John Torrence's R&D facility had been the most innovative laboratory in its industry.

—Federal Engineering and High Technology Products remained the high-quality producers in their industries but made no headway as they tried to diversify into systems businesses.

—AT&T developed an optimal organization to deliver low-cost, high-quality universal telephone service. Yet, its prior success seems to be an impediment as AT&T moves into unregulated environments.

—Amity Bank had been a top performer in traditional banking products and services. While it remained preeminent in its traditional services, it was making no headway in its development of coordinated product/service packages to distinct markets.

In each of these examples, the managers and their respective organizations are used to success. Their histories are rooted in success. Yet they all have experienced crisis, the frustration of mediocre performance and the pressure to find organizational solutions to novel strategic challenges. In each case, organization design is a necessary but not sufficient condition for organizational renewal. Each organization is in transition—a transition in which it must become a fundamentally different kind of organization. To some extent, these transformations are predictable. In each case they can be managed. Quite apart from designing and changing organizations to compete in the short run, this chapter focuses on designing organizations to be effective over the various stages of a product class life cycle. We move from organizational statics to dynamics, focusing on patterns in organizational evolution and the role of strategic design over time.

Chapters 4 through 10 concentrate on designing organizations to accomplish a set of tasks, which, in turn, help accomplish a set of strategic objectives. However, competitive environments change. As environments change, so too must organization strategy. Firms that do not adapt to environmental shifts underperform and eventually fail (e.g., the demise of the vacuum tube industry after semiconductors). Management in Medtek's laboratory, Federal Engineering, High Technology Products, and AT&T were coping with implementing new strategies. In each example, changing competitive, legal, political, or technological conditions required fresh strategic responses. As strategy is the driving factor in our organizational model (Chapter 2) and is the primary determinant in strategic design (Chapter 5), shifts in strategy must have a profound range of organizational effects.

However, changing strategic objectives is never sufficient; organizations need to effectively implement those revised strategies. These transformations require changes not only in strategic design but throughout the organization. The issue of organizational evolution brings strategic design back into our full organizing model. Each of our case studies requires changes not only in strategic design but in almost every other major aspect of the organization.

This chapter deals with organizing over time. It focuses on managing for stability and managing fundamental change; we move from organizational statics to organizational dynamics. We trace sources of organizational inertia, discuss generic forces for fundamental change, and develop a transformational approach to organizational evolution. These ideas on organizational evolution indicate that strategic design is never fully accomplished (except for those organizations embedded in perfectly stable environments). Such ideas also provide insight into the impact of organizational history, politics, and executive leadership on strategic design; on the necessity of building consistencies between strategic design, individuals, and the informal organization and organization arrangements over time; and on the differential nature of change requirements as organizations evolve.

# ORGANIZATIONS AND THEIR ENVIRONMENTS: STRATEGIC CHOICES

Organizations must develop social and technical systems to accomplish tasks and meet strategic objectives. Organizational success involves choosing appropriate objectives and developing a congruency between tasks, individuals, organization arrangements, and the informal organization—of doing the right things and doing them well. Inappropriate strategies assure organizational failure—even if well implemented. For example, organizations that still make mechanical cash registers must suffer in a semiconductor-oriented market. Similarly, memory firms that are committed to bubble memory must either switch to semiconductor memory or exit the industry. Strategy is the initial, most primary, strategic choice.

Appropriate strategy is a necessary but not sufficient condition for organization effectiveness. Management must build social and technical systems to accomplish strategy. Choices must be made regarding work and work flows, individuals, culture, and organization arrangements. These choices must, in turn, be congruent with work demands and be internally consistent (see Chapter 2). For example, after Theodore Vail established AT&T's strategy of universal, low-cost service, he and his successors developed a completely congruent social and technical system in service of the corporation's strategy: they hired and developed "Bell-shaped" employees, shaped the Ma Bell culture, and developed an elaborate functional organization. Through more than sixty years of incremental change, AT&T's management developed the optimal organization to meet its fixed strategy.

Organization design hinges on strategy; strategic grouping is driven solely by strategy (moderated by political and historical dynamics). Different organization forms are better suited for different strategies (Chapter 5). Strategic linking follows from strategic grouping and is driven by work-related interdependence. More complex strategies build on more complex interdependencies and therefore require more complex formal linking mechanisms (Chapter 6). Similarly, different strategies require fundamentally different organization cultures. Those me-first, technology-driven firms must have a different set of core values and norms than me-too, marketing organizations (Chapter 9). Not all organization designs are equally effective. The choices of strategic design make an economic difference; strategic grouping, formal linking, and organization culture all must meet critical strategic contingencies and work requirements.

Organization designs are never perfect; for a given strategy, the managerial challenge is to incrementally adjust strategic grouping, linking, and culture to be more congruent with strategic and work requirements. For example, Laffer's technology transfer problem in Chapter 6 amounted to coming up with a relatively minor structural adjustment and a focused cultural change (around technological collaboration).

Assuming an appropriate strategy, managers must incrementally adjust systems, procedures, controls, and individuals so they become ever more congruent. These incremental changes and adjustments in the system can be carried out by all levels of the organization. At General Radio, fifty years of incremental adaptation resulted in an engineering-dominated, simple functional organization with a rich variety of committee and task forces and a culture that valued engineering and quality products. Incremental adjustments in General Radio's systems and procedures were initiated by middle- and lower-level managers, guided by the vision of the firm as espoused by the founder and carried forward by ensuing General Radio executives.

## CONSEQUENCES OF SUCCESS: STRUCTURAL AND SOCIAL INERTIA

Managers who choose appropriate strategies, adopt appropriate strategic designs, and, in turn, shape consistent cultures and hire and train the right set of human resources, will have highly effective organizations. Congruence between social and structural organizational factors is associated with effective performance in the short run, as well as with structural and social inertia. Organizational inertia is a self-reinforcing pattern in which social and structural characteristics become progressively more complexly interlinked. This complexity begets more complexity and ever greater internal momentum, reinforcing the current strategic orientation. In every one of our vignettes, the managers had to deal with the inertia of past successes' constraining current attempts to change organizational strategy.

Organizational success and its correlates of size and time drive organizational inertia. As organizations become more successful, they become larger and must handle increased demand and increased volume. To handle increased size and volume, organizations must become more formalized. Systems, procedures, and processes become more formalized and interlinked to handle increased work flows. At General Radio, the shift to more standard product lines and a growth emphasis required much more attention to systems, procedures, and controls within and between each area of the firm. Similarly, whereas automobiles used to be made in flexible job shops at Ford Motor Company, the rise of assembly lines and Henry Ford's emphasis on cost and volume was associated with rigid work flows, standards, rules, and regulations that directed all aspects of the organization's operations. Automotive firms with a strategy of low volume/high cost (e.g., Rolls Royce) did not evolve the rigid organization required at Ford.

Increased size and increased work flows require more bureaucratic structures and systems. These more bureaucratic systems are, in turn, relatively inflexible systems. Increases in efficiency are directly related to decreased flexibility or increased structural inertia. For example, Henry Ford's assembly line system at River Rouge had a four-day inventory turn and produced a finished Model T in two and one half hours. These efficiencies cut the cost of a Model T from over $3000 to under $500. However, these enormous efficiencies were also associated with great structural rigidities. Ford was unable to incrementally adapt the Model T to the fully enclosed automobiles of General Motors. Ford was forced to close down River Rouge, lay off thousands of employees, and completely retool to produce fully enclosed cars. The link between size, volume, standardization, and inflexibility is quite general and can be readily experienced in restaurants, retail businesses, and universities (among other industries).

Organizational success is also associated with increasing organizational age; successful organizations get older. Increased organizational age generates emergent social forces for stability. As individuals remain in positions and as groups age, they work to stabilize and routinize their environments. Whereas individuals show remarkable innovation early in their careers, later on they direct much more energy toward maintaining and routinizing work relations. Similarly, as groups age, they too invest progressively more creativity in controlling and stabilizing work relations.

Individual and group social inertia is generated by commitment processes at the individual level and by conformity-generating processes within and between groups. The enormous resistance faced by Laffer (Chapter 6) was generated by key individuals personally committed to the rightness of previous courses of action who saw the technology transfer board as just another organizational diversion. Similarly, the "not-invented-here" syndrome, so common in technology-based groups, reflects social and group commitments to their own, local views of technology and the marketplace.

Organizations also become more inertial as they age. Organizations evolve standard operating procedures, socialization processes, precedent, history, and culture, which stabilize work relations within and between groups. For example, fifty years of history at Federal Engineering resulted in a myriad of norms, values, and social structures that reinforced and perpetuated the "Federal Engineering way." Similarly, AT&T developed a rich informal organization rooted in the core values of universal service, quality, and engineering. The Ma Bell culture provided enormous certainty as to appropriate behavior at every level of the Bell System.

The longer these emergent social relations evolve, the richer and more complex they become. These social and historical forces for stability are, in turn, related to (and partly shaped by) increased structural complexity. These internal social and structural forces for inertia become more complex over time. They can be further accentuated if directly linked to a set of core values. To the extent that individuals and groups attach meaning and value to their work, they become more committed to their behavior. The clarity and importance of service and quality at AT&T helped Ma Bell employees better understand their work and its relation to the firm and to the larger society. These core values helped focus behavior and helped individuals understand their behaviors. Work behavior anchored by core values and history results in substantial energy to transmit and perpetuate those behaviors and core values.

Social and structural inertia is a double-edged sword. At times, this inertia is profoundly functional. At other times, it is a fundamental threat to the organization's existence. Organizational inertia is a positive force as long as a firm's strategy is appropriate and the firm is successful. Social and structural inertia provides added energy and intensity in accomplishing the organization's work. This inertia provides the social glue — via precedent, history, and informal relations — that accomplishes work even in the face of ambiguity, shortages in resources, and threat. This social inertia, this convergence about "how we get things done here," helped make AT&T, Federal Engineering, and Amity Bank successful.

However, if environments change in a fundamental fashion or if strategies change, then this social or structural inertia is an important impediment to change. Inertial organizations are relatively closed systems. They often have ineffective environmental scanning mechanisms as managers attend more and more to familiar informational sources. Worse, highly inertial systems tend to act counterproductively in the face of environmental threat. Managers rely even more on standard processes under high-stress conditions. Executives frequently escalate their commitments to previously successful courses of action. Vigilant search is sharply curtailed in inertial organizations that face some external threat.

The combination of decreased information, decreased problem-solving effectiveness, and increased personal commitments to prior courses of action are seeds of disaster when environments change. For example, the demise of the *Saturday Evening Post* illustrates the lack of awareness of editorial trends and the belated, counterproductive efforts to turn around the distinguished magazine. Similarly, the response of large, older, dominant firms to technological threat is stark. In industry after industry, new technologies are ignored by the dominant firms, only to be introduced by new entrants. The airline, telegraph, locomotive, lighting, vacuum tube, television, steel, typewriter, and calculator industries are examples in which dominant firms ignored new technologies. In each case, the dominant firms increased their emphasis on the technologies they knew best and so, were replaced.

Initial processes arise in all organizations. These inherent social processes become more entrenched in larger, older organizations and are accentuated in high-performing organizations. These inherent inertial processes are profoundly functional as long as competitive environments are stable but can be just as dysfunctional if competitive environments change.

## ENVIRONMENTAL CHANGE: EXTERNAL FORCES FOR FUNDAMENTAL CHANGE

Competitive conditions are shaped by changes in demand; technologies; and legal, political, and social factors. While industry patterns differ, there are stages in the evolution of product classes that have major strategic implications for organizations. These stages in product class evolution require fundamentally different strategies and, in turn, different types of organizations.

In emerging product classes, there is substantial uncertainty about technologies, products, and markets. For example, in the early days of computers, it was unclear just what computers were, who the relevant markets might be, and what the relevant technologies for these new products were. Similarly, when automobiles were introduced at the turn of the century, there were no clear markets, and numerous technologies and products were competing to meet transportation needs (e.g., gas-driven versus coal-fired versus wood-burning versus electric engines).

During the opening of a product class, firms compete based on functional performance. What kind of car, copying machine, computer, airframe, or typewriter performs the job better? Rapid product innovation is important as firms learn from experience. Cost is not an issue, as firms are highly sensitive to the customized needs of early users. Organizations tend to be small, functionally organized, and dominated by development and/or marketing functions, with a loose, entrepreneurial, fast-paced culture. Organizations in emerging product classes tend to be dominated by powerful entrepreneurs who run me-first kinds of organizations (see Figures 11-1, 11-2, and 11-3).

As a product class evolves, demand increases rapidly and new entrants emerge. The competition between product types (e.g., what type of engine to power automobiles, what form of typewriter, what operating system, or what word size in the early minicomputer market [2, 4, 6, 8, 10 bit]) eventually leads to industry standardization. At some point, due either to technological or marketing dominance, one or two standard product forms evolve. For example, in the airline industry, the emergence

FIGURE 11-1     Changing Rates of Product and Process Innovation

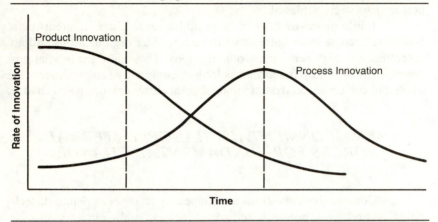

Source: Adapted from W. Abernathy and J. Utterback, "Patterns of Industrial Innovation," *Technology Review* 80 (June 1978): 2–9.

of the DC-3 gave rise to complete standardization for twenty years (until jets). The Fordson tractor, Smith Model 5 typewriter, and IBM 360 series are other examples of dominant designs that shaped their respective industries.

The emergence of an industry standard or dominant design has important strategic implications. It signals a shift in strategic emphasis from major product innovation to more incremental product change and major process innovation. Organizations then begin to segment markets based on incremental product differences and reduced costs. Given more standardized products, firms must invest in process innovation to make those more standard products more efficiently. Marketing, R&D, and production all must increase in importance during this phase of a product class' evolution. Because new markets open, organization design must become more complex as the degree of organization specialization and work interdependence increases. Further, because of increased volume and size demands, the organization must be much more professionally run than earlier entrepreneurial organizations (review Figures 11-1 and 11-3).

As the rate of demand levels or decreases, the basis of competition shifts again. In mature product classes, firms compete based on cost, efficiencies, and incremental product and process innovation. While the mature phase of a product class may be quite profitable, the bases of success hinge on efficiency, standardization, and innovative marketing and sales. For example, in the cigarette industry, firms compete based on process innovation, cost, and incremental product innovation. The R&D that does occur is oriented toward process improvements; marketing and production tend to be the dominant functions.

FIGURE 11-2    Changing Strategic Contingencies

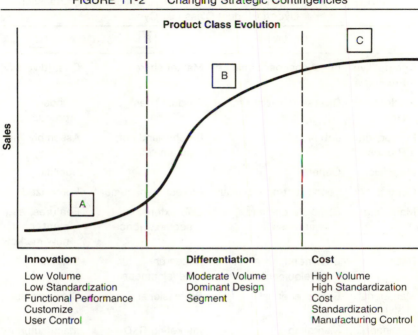

**Product Class Evolution**

| Innovation | Differentiation | Cost |
|---|---|---|
| Low Volume | Moderate Volume | High Volume |
| Low Standardization | Dominant Design | High Standardization |
| Functional Performance | Segment | Cost |
| Customize | | Standardization |
| User Control | | Manufacturing Control |

During the mature phase of a product class, firms work to standardize their product lines and invest in incremental product and process changes. Manufacturing is capital intensive and relies more on standardized materials and machinery. These organizations are large, functionally organized, and bureaucratic; they do not produce radical product innovation, and their cultures emphasize stability, formality, and cost (review Figures 11-1, 11-2, and 11-3).

Beyond technological change, product class conditions are also shaped by changes in political, legal, and social events. For example, changes in factor prices, regulatory constraints, and national/international law may have an enormous impact on competition within industries. Airlines and the financial services industries have each gone through fluctuating periods of regulation, even as their respective core technologies were changing. While any industry will have its unique history and different rates of change in technology, legal, and social factors, product class conditions are not static. As product class conditions change, so, too, do dominant competitive issues.

As product classes evolve, organizations must compete based on fundamentally different strategic contingencies; the type of strategic innovation shifts from product, to process, to incremental product/process innovation. Because strategies must shift over time, so too must organi-

FIGURE 11-3    Organizing Over Time: Organizational Characteristics
Over a Product Class Life Cycle

|  | A | B | C |
|---|---|---|---|
| Competitive Emphasis | Functional performance | Market share | Cost/(diversify) |
| Product Line | Diverse, customized | Product lines | Standard product |
| Production Process | Job shop | Batch/islands of automation | Assembly line |
| Materials | General |  | Specific |
| Control | Loose, entrepreneurial | Project management | Formalized |
| Marketing | Stimulate demand, awareness | Line extension segment, price | Features, segment, cost, new markets |
| R&D | User need, development | Research, development | Service |
| Managerial Style | Entrepreneurial | Professional | Stewardship |
| Dominant Function | Marketing/ entrepreneurial | Marketing/R&D | Manufacturing/ sales/ marketing |
| Size | Small |  | Large |
| Growth | Rapid | Moderate | Slow |

Source: Adapted from W. Abernathy and J. Utterback, "Patterns of Industrial Innovation," *Technology Review* 80 (June 1978): 2–9.

zations. Strategies, structure, people, processes, and culture must change as a product class evolves. For example, AT&T was founded as American Bell. This early telephone company was a small entrepreneurial firm dominated by R&D with no manufacturing or distribution facilities. After the emergence of a dominant design in telephones and telephonic transmission, a new AT&T management team, headed by Theodore Vail, transformed AT&T into the large, standardized, functional organization that remained essentially stable through the 1970s. As the AT&T example illustrates, legal and political factors interact to shape strategic contingencies within product classes. Lawrence and Dyer[1] describe the nature of product class evolution and organization evolution in a host of industries, including steel, automobile, banking, hospital, education, and computers.

If product class conditions change, organizational strategies and, in turn, organizations themselves must change. As strategic contingencies shift from product innovation, to process innovation and segmentation, to standardization and cost, organizations must transform themselves from one type of organization to another (review Figures 11-2 and 11-3). Organizations that compete over a product class must become different kinds of organizations from what they were. Strategy, structure, culture, and processes must change. Those strategies and organizational characteristics that are appropriate during one product class stage are dysfunctional in the next. Paradoxically, the factors that made AT&T, Federal Engineering, Amity Bank, and Medtek so successful were, in time, seeds of disaster.

Environmental shifts that lead to fundamental strategic shifts occur when a dominant design emerges, when substitute technologies are developed (tubes versus semiconductors), and/or when there are legal, political, or social shocks to an industry (oil prices or regulation). While it is unclear when and how competitive contingencies will change, we know that they do.

Given the difficulties in managing system-wide change, most firms fail to make these strategic reorientations. While many firms enter emerging industries, most do not survive the shake-out (review stage A-B in Figure 11-2). Similarly, most dominant firms have enormous difficulty in hosting new entrepreneurial ventures (review stage C-A in Figure 11-2). Whether the problem is one of an entrepreneurial firm's making the transformation to a professionally oriented firm or of a mature firm's attempting to effectively host entrepreneurial ventures, the fundamental problem is the same—that of managing strategies, structure, culture, and individuals in order to cope with changing competitive demands.

## PATTERNS IN ORGANIZATIONAL EVOLUTION

Organizations generate powerful internal forces for stability. These inherent forces, along with appropriate strategic designs, systems, and human resources, are associated with organization effectiveness as long as competitive conditions are not fundamentally altered. When environments do change, strategy must change and prior organization structures and cultures may no longer be functional. Organizations do not make these strategic transformations smoothly. Rather, given social and structural inertia, organizations either do not change and are then trapped by these inertial forces, or they make these transformations in discontinuous leaps. For example, whereas the *Saturday Evening Post* never changed, Prime Computer, after four years of constant growth with a strategy of high-priced, "Cadillac" computers, changed its strategy, structure, and systems all at once in 1975. Prime's strategy shifted to one of lower-priced minis and systems sold to end users. This transformation required different structures, systems, and a modified culture. Under a new set of managers, Prime engaged in yet another strategic shift in 1981 — diversifying into robotics and CAD/CAM.

Organizational transformations involve discontinuous and simultaneous changes throughout the organization. Strategy changes along with strategic and operational design. These changes are also associated with discontinuous changes in power and controls. Again at Prime, the strategy shift to low-priced minicomputers and systems was also associated with a bolstering of the power of sales and a diminution in the power of R&D. Controls were also established to track costs and sales more carefully. Similarly, at General Radio the shift to a high-growth, marketing-oriented instrument business signaled the demise of "the engineer is king" mentality. Power, control, and systems shifted to product line managers, and General Radio's structure changed from a simple functional structure to a relatively complex project organization. These system-wide changes were all initiated simultaneously.

Such organizational transformations define periods in the life of a firm. Within these periods, organizations build structures, systems, and cultures to accomplish particular strategies. Managers incrementally adjust structures, values, norms, and practices to gain the benefits of increased congruence (and increased inertia) between technical and social organizational components. These convergent periods are not static. Rather, highly effective transformations are characterized by periods of numerous incremental changes and adaptations to achieve greater internal congruence. Implementing change during these periods engenders relatively few individual, political, or control problems.

Convergent periods are punctuated by metamorphic changes. Strategic reorientations involve simultaneous changes in strategy and in structures, processes, and senior management. Strategic reorientation involves redesigning the social and technical aspects of organizations at once. For example, Joe Flavin at Singer is attempting to transform this old-line sewing machine organization into a high-technology aerospace firm by simultaneously changing structure, processes, key managers, and controls. Similarly, Hewlett-Packard is attempting to diversify and become a more marketing-oriented firm via major changes in structure (from functional to market-based organization), managers, culture (from engineering-focused to market- and engineering-focused), and internal processes.

Reorientations are always traumatic, as they involve simultaneous changes in strategy, structure, power, and controls. These are changes of the system, rather than changes in the system. Individuals experience the shock of suddenly working in "a different organization." At General

Radio, such wholesale changes were also associated with a change in the firm's name to GenRad. Not only did employees come back to a new structure, strategy, systems, and set of managers, the name of their organization changed. These changes are even more traumatic when they also involve core values (as they did at GenRad).

As organizations evolve through these discontinuities, so too does strategic organization design. Shifts in strategic groupings do not occur in a set fashion. Rather, they are driven by changes in organization strategy, which, in turn, reflects changes in competitive conditions.

As strategic grouping changes, so too must strategic linking, organization culture, and operational design. Management must choose appropriate structures to meet strategic requirements and build complementary social and operational systems to do the work. These organizational transformations, then, represent more than changes in structure; they represent major changes in strategic grouping, linking, operational design, culture, and often management, all in the service of a new organization strategy.

Organizations evolve through periods demarked by discontinuous metamorphic changes. Convergent periods are characterized by incremental change in strategic and operational design and in corresponding systems and processes in the service of a given strategy. During convergent periods, executive management attends to culture and core values, while middle management incrementally adjusts structures and processes toward greater internal consistency. Convergent periods are punctuated by changes in strategy and simultaneous changes in structures, systems, and processes. These reorientations lead to the next convergent period—one of incrementally adjusting organization design and cultures to the new strategy. Changing environmental conditions do not cause reorientations. Highly effective organizations engage in reorientations that correspond to environmental conditions. Low performing organizations will either not reorient when environmental conditions change or will engage in too many reorientations.

This period-based perspective on organizational evolution highlights the importance of organizational history, effective change management, and the role of executive leadership in designing organizations. Reorientations make salient organization history and precedent as they represent a clear break from prior courses of action and represent a new social and organizational order. The longer the convergent period, the more entrenched the organization's culture and the stronger the structural and social inertial forces. As history is embodied in stories, myths, heroes, and an entrenched political system, these transformations always involve coping with the legacy of organizational history and dealing with the politics and personalities in change management. For example, the managers at Medtek, Federal Engineering, High Technology Products, AT&T,

and Occidental Petroleum all must deal with the histories, personalities, and organizational characteristics of the past as they attempt to change strategies, structures, and cultures in their respective firms.

Implementing change is a critical issue in strategic reorientation. Since reorientations are systemic changes, management must make a consistent set of changes in tasks, individuals, organization arrangements, and informal organization. Because these changes represent a discontinuous shift from prior courses of action, reorientations will always involve substantial individual and political resistance to change and enormous problems in control (see Chapter 10). Implementing these metamorphic changes may require simultaneous sharp changes throughout the organization, with relatively little direct participation by middle- and lower-level management. New executives from outside of the organization may also be required. Although senior management can delegate those incremental changes that frequently occur within convergent periods, they cannot delegate changes involved in reorientations. Senior management must take personal responsibility for implementing strategic reorientation. For example, at GenRad, wholesale changes were initiated in a very short period, directed by relatively few senior managers (many new to GenRad).

Organization history and core values assume a particularly important role in implementing strategic reorientations. When management can build on the organization's history and core values, strategic reorientations will be less traumatic than when history is ignored or when prior core values are rejected. To the extent that management can build on history and core values to be consistent with current strategic contingencies, the organization will have a base from which to build a new social and technical order. For example, while IBM has evolved through several strategic reorientations (e.g., its transformation into a computer company and 360 decision), its trilogy of core values has remained an anchor of stability.

Reorientations that also involve changes in core values (e.g., General Radio, Singer, AT&T) are much more traumatic in that core values and history are an anchor to an obsolete past. Tightly held values and a proud history are sources of enormous individual and political resistance as individuals and groups attempt to hold on to the past. Reorientations that also involve changes in core values require sustained executive attention to shaping a new or revised set of core values and to reinterpreting and re-creating a new organizational ideology. At the Singer and Harris Corporations, for example, the respective management teams must not only make decisions regarding strategy, tasks, individuals, structures, and systems; they must also shape new cultures and ideologies as these historically low-technology firms attempt to transform themselves into high-technology organizations.

Executive leadership assumes a particularly important role in this metamorphic approach to organizational evolution. Executives must make choices as to strategy, strategic grouping and linking, and organization culture, but they must also decide when and how to engage in these transformations. Whereas many executives can choose appropriate structures, systems, and processes for a given strategy, relatively few executives have the vision to initiate organizational transformations short of being forced to do so by crisis.

Organizations tend to be forced into these metamorphic changes either by crises or through major changes in the executive team. The most successful executives have not only the technical and social skills to manage organizations but the visionary insight to know when and how to engage in organizational transformations. William Thurston at GenRad; David Dunn at Prime; Thomas Watson, Jr., at IBM; Walter Wriston at Citibank; and William Hewlett and David Packard at HP are each examples of visionary executives who led internally driven transformations of their respective firms. Whether through external succession or by the existing management team, executive leadership must manage for consistency during convergent periods and engage in and manage transformations when environmental conditions demand. We return to the role and importance of executive leadership in Chapter 12.

## SUMMARY

Strategic organization design involves important choices in the areas of strategic grouping, structural linking, operational design, and organizational culture. However, an appropriate organization design is a necessary but not sufficient condition for organizational effectiveness. Organization design must be bolstered with an informal organization, formal systems and processes, and appropriate human resources to accomplish organizational strategy. Organization design is, then, one important piece in the larger problem of building effective organizations.

This chapter has explored the consequences of building consistencies between strategy, design, organizational processes, and individuals. Consistency, or congruence, is associated with effective performance and organizational inertia. Inertia facilitates organization processes as long as strategy does not change. If strategy changes, social and structural inertia becomes an impediment to organizational change. Congruence is, then, a double-edged sword. It is vital for the success of a particular strategy but is a source of conflict, politics, and individual resistance to change if an organization attempts to adjust to environmental demands.

Competitive environments do change. Environmental change is

sometimes driven by patterned changes in product classes (i.e., dominant design and/or technological substitution) or exogenous shocks (i.e., legal, political, or social events). Whatever the source of environmental change, the challenge is to manage the transformation of the organization. Given inertial processes at all organizational levels, organizations do not make strategic shifts smoothly. Rather, they evolve through metamorphic, or transformational, changes. The transformations of IBM, Ford, Medtek, Hewlett-Packard, Prime, Singer, and General Radio are not extreme cases. They typify the systemic changes required to implement new strategies.

Organizations evolve through periods of incremental change punctuated by transformational change. During convergent periods, managers incrementally adjust grouping choices, linking mechanisms, operational design, and organizational processes to fit strategic requirements. During organizational transformations, strategy, design, cultures, and processes change simultaneously. These transformations lead to the next convergent period — one of incremental adjustments to structure, systems, and informal processes. Organization design is, then, never fully accomplished. During convergent periods, management make minor adjustments over time. During organizational transformations, however, organization design must be totally reshaped to meet new strategic requirements. These major design changes require complementary changes in the informal organization and in the organization's human resource characteristics.

Whether forced by crisis or initiated proactively, organizational transformations must be driven by executive leadership. Only senior management can deal with the systemic resistance to change that all transformations generate. Metamorphic change is experienced by employees as inconsistent with the organization's past, as violating core values. Transformational change creates increased awareness of organizational history and precedent and triggers political and individual resistance to change. Organizational transformations that can build on existing core values and history, even as structures, systems, and processes change, will be less traumatic than transformations that also change core values. Therefore, change management is a vital issue in designing organizations over time.

Given strong inertial forces for stability, organizations will not usually reform themselves from within as environments change. Organizational transformations will either occur after a prolonged crisis, during which the organization is forced to change, or they may proactively occur driven by visionary executive leadership. Beyond the traditional consequential choices of strategy, design, culture, and human resources, executive leadership must also make the decision to initiate and actively implement these organizational transformations. The challenge is, then, to manage for organizational stability and take advantage of social and structural inertia as well as to be sensitive enough to environmental events to be prepared to initiate and implement strategic reorientations. Managers must prepare to design and redesign their firms as product class conditions unfold.

## NOTES

1. We build on a substantial literature on organization adaptation, including W. Abernathy and J. Utterback, "Patterns of Industrial Innovation," *Technology Review* 80 (June 1978): 2–9; A. Cooper and D. Schendel, "Strategic Responses to Technological Threats," *Business Horizon* (1976); J. Galbraith and D. Nathanson, *Strategy Implementation: The Role of Structure and Process*, (New York: West, 1978); R. Hall, "A System Pathology of an Organization," *Administrative Science Quarterly* 21 (1976): 185–211; K. Harrigan, *Strategic Flexibility*, (Lexington, MA: Lexington Books, 1985); R. Katz, "Time and Work: Toward an Integrative Perspective," in B. Staw and L. Cummings, eds., *Research in Organization Behavior*, vol. 2, (Greenwich, CT: JAI Press, 1980); P. Lawrence and D. Dyer, *Reviewing American Industry*, (New York: Free Press, 1983); M. Maidique, "Entrepreneurs, Champions and Technological Innovation," *Sloan Management Review* 21 (1980): 59–76; B. Staw, L. Sandelands, and J. Dutton, "Threat-Rigidity Effects in Organizational Behavior," *Administrative Science Quarterly* 26 (1981): 501–24; M. Tushman and E. Romanelli, "Organizational Evolution: A Metamorphosis Model of Convergence and Reorientation," in B. Staw and L. Cummings, eds., *Research in Organizational Behavior* vol. 7, (Greenwich, CT: JAI Press, 1985), 171–222; M. Tushman, W. Newman, and E. Romanelli, "Convergence and Upheaval: Managing the Unsteady Pace of Organizational Evolution," *California Management Review* (Winter 1986); M. Tushman, B. Virany, and E. Romanelli, "Executive Succession, Strategic Reorientations and Organization Evolution," *Technology in Society* 7 (1985): 297–313.

# 12

# A Summary of
# Design Concepts

This book has attempted to provide insight into organization design. It has approached the topic from a managerial perspective, focusing on the types of questions, dilemmas, and decisions that managers face.

In this book, we have constructed a way of thinking about organization design. We began with a model of organizational performance as a general view of the elements involved in creating and managing effective organizations. Within the context of that general model, we outlined an approach to organization design, beginning with a definition of design, a review of the information-processing perspective, and an application of that perspective to the key design decisions of determining organizational groupings and creating coordination mechanisms. We then used the information-processing approach in a step-by-step sequence for making design decisions. Finally, in Chapters 9, 10, and 11, we focused on some key issues that should be considered in making and implementing design decisions. First, we talked about the informal organization and the concept of organizational culture, which led to a discussion of the problems of implementing change. We then took a long-term perspective and discussed the issue of designing organizations over time and the related question of organization evolution.

In this final chapter, we will briefly reemphasize some themes that have run throughout this book. In addition, we will draw on the concept of organizations over time presented in Chapter 11 and link it specifically to design decisions that managers face at different points in time. Third, we will discuss the limitations of organization design as a managerial tool. Finally, we will close with some perspectives on the role of "executive leadership" in organization design.

## *KEY OBSERVATIONS*

In Chapter 1, we shared some views of the role of design in the management of organizations. We can now revisit these views and add some observations that have been made in the course of subsequent chapters:

**Organization design is a potentially powerful managerial tool.** While an organization is made up of various components (task, individual, informal organization, and formal organizational arrangements), the manager has a limited ability to directly modify or manipulate all of these. Design is a key managerial tool because it is amenable to direct change and because it can impact other organization components (such as individual skills or the formation of informal organization arrangements). A design change is a valuable substantive and symbolic form of action. The value of design is not only in its content but also in the messages sent through redesign.

**Organization design is a continuous activity.** Part of a manager's job is to make continual design decisions. In an organization that operates in relatively uncertain environments, it is natural to expect frequent adjustments in its design. In one sense, the design is always being "fine-tuned." The implication is that day-to-day actions shape the structure of the organization, and therefore these decisions should be guided by a systematic way of thinking about the resulting organization design.

**Design decisions need to balance strategic and human perspectives.** We have argued that there are two different ways of thinking about design decisions. One way sees the organization as a mechanistic device to be designed solely to achieve its mission (or in our terms, to support strategy and be congruent with the task). Another view is more organic and sees design as a way of arranging human interaction and relationships. In this view, design evolves to meet the needs of individuals or groups in response to people's concerns, political factors, evolution of a culture, and so on. Obviously, neither of these views is solely sufficient for building effective organizations. This needed balance of perspectives is generally seen in our organization performance model and specifically reflected in the concept of fit, or congruence. Effective designs balance the requirement to support strategy with the human realities and consequences of various ways of organizing.

**Design decisions should balance scientific and pragmatic concerns.** The information-processing theory pushes managers toward certain types of design decisions. However, design decisions should take into account the very pragmatic concerns of cost, feasibility, politics, and organizational inertia. The approaches we have proposed here attempt to balance the scientific view with the pragmatic view to provide a set of tools that are both scientifically based and useful.

**Design decisions can become more effective through the use of systematic processes or approaches.** Clearly, managers can make more effective design decisions if they work through a systematic series of steps for thinking about those decisions. The need for systematic thinking should not be confused with the explicitness of the process. One might envision the design sequence as being used with a design team meeting for intensive sessions, gathering large amounts of data, and working through each step in the decision-making sequence. Indeed, there are some times when such an explicit, intensive process is necessary. On the other hand, our approach could also be applied by an individual manager who spends an hour organizing the data that he or she already has and thinking through the various options. A systematic approach is used in both cases. The time spent on such an approach is a wise investment, particularly when compared with the costs of trial-and-error approaches to organization design.

## INCREMENTAL VERSUS METAMORPHIC DESIGNS

In Chapter 11, we outlined a view of organizational evolution. Relatively long periods of continuous and incremental change are punctuated by shorter periods of discontinuous and much more profound changes—metamorphic changes that affect the fundamental nature, shape, and identity of an organization.

While we have talked about a whole set of changes in this discussion (strategy, organization design, organizational culture, people, and so on), there is a clear message for the manager/organization designer. As previously mentioned, design decisions are made every day. These are incremental design decisions that, over time, shape the organization. However, the goal of these design changes (be it a new assignment to a single manager or the reorganization of an operating division) is to maintain the congruence, and consistency of the organizational system. As minor changes occur in the environment, or as an organization grows in size and scope, the design is altered to maintain fit with the strategy, task, individuals, and informal organization. There come times in the life of an organization, however, when major metamorphic reorientations or re-creations must occur. In these cases, the goal of redesign is not to fine-tune, adjust, or maintain congruence. Rather, the redesign is part of a larger, more intensive change of form.

Design may play different roles in different situations. In some cases, the design may play a supporting role. A new strategy, leadership team, set of values, and operating style may have already been initiated, and the redesign is done to support and solidify these changes. In other cases, design may have a leading role. An organization redesign may be used to initiate a change process. In such cases, a design might purposely be created not to fit with the rest of the organization. The manager/designer might redesign to create turbulence, to shape people out of their ways of doing things, and to orient people in different directions. In this case, the goal is to create movement in the system toward a new balance or fit. Thus, the design analysis (design criteria, information-processing needs, and impact analysis) should focus on the organization's desired future state rather than on its present course.

## THE LIMITATIONS OF DESIGN

Throughout our discussion, we have focused on the potential power of design as a tool. We have emphasized the possible great impact (positive or negative) of a design decision on the way in which an organization functions. In part, we have done this to underscore the importance of making these decisions in an informed and systematic manner.

However, it would be a great mistake to think of organization design as an all-powerful tool. Situations do occur in which redesigns have virtually no impact on organizational patterns of behavior and activity. In certain situations and conditions, design is merely cosmetic. Why is this so? Part of the answer lies in our organization performance model. While we have emphasized the formal organization arrangements portion of the model, other components may also be as influential or more influential than the formal structures or processes. The strategy and the task make profound demands on the organization, and individual members of the organization greatly influence patterns of activity through the expression of their needs, expectations, skills, experiences, knowledge, and feelings. Finally, the informal organization—including culture, informal working arrangements, patterns of leadership, power, and informal groups—also has a profound impact on behavior.

The informal organization is, in fact, the key to understanding the impact, or lack of impact, of design. In different organizations, the formal (versus the informal) arrangements may have a different degree of salience. Usually, the resulting behavior is a product of both informal and formal arrangements. However, organizations have traditions, cultures, and norms that may either support or undercut the impact of the formal organization. In some cases, for example, the formal organization arrangements may be very salient because the culture holds them in high regard (an example of this is in military organizations). In other cases, the operating style may not support the formal arrangements, or the actual practice may be to deemphasize the formal design (examples of this can be seen in new ventures, small high-technology organizations, and research and development organizations). In these cases, behavior is largely governed by the informal system, and design changes in the formal organization arrangements may have little impact. Similarly, when leaders systematically ignore the formal processes, design changes may be of little consequence.

Thus, design must be considered in context. A design change that is very effective in one setting may have little effect in another. Again, we come back to the need to balance the technical and human perspectives and to diagnose prior to initiating change.

## LEADERSHIP AND STRATEGIC CHANGE

Ultimately, the shaping of organizations is part of the role of executive leadership — those who are charged with providing the most senior-level direction of an organization (or a major component or business unit of an organization). The executive can use organization design, along with other tools, to build effectiveness incrementally over time and, when necessary, to bring about significant metamorphic changes.

This book has been about organization design, not about leadership per se. However, in building on the view of organizations (both statically and over time) that we have discussed in this book, we can identify several key tasks that are critical to effective executive leadership:

**Having a strategic vision of the organization.** Perhaps the most critical demand on the executive is to develop a vision of his or her organization's strategic position within a competitive industry environment. It is ultimately the job of the leader (obviously helped by others) to determine what the organization will become, how it will compete, and what it must do to be successful.

**Understanding growth dynamics and types of change.** The leader also needs to understand the industrial/environmental context of his or her organization. That understanding is critical in order to recognize those situations in which strategic choice is required. The executive must be able to recognize when incremental strategic or organizational changes are appropriate, as opposed to those situations that demand metamorphic change.

**Making the right strategic choices.** When faced with the need for metamorphic shifts, the leader must make the right strategic choices. Managers face many strategic decisions over the course of their careers, but strategic choices made at points of metamorphic change are frequently watershed events that determine the course of an organization for years.

**Making the right design choices.** The leader needs to make design choices that support the direction of the strategic choices he or she has made. Such design choices include both the specifics of organization design and the larger "system design" task of shaping the informal organization, task, and individual components of the organization.

**Implementing changes effectively.** Having determined strategic and design choices, the leader is then faced with the challenge of implementing those choices — bringing about significant and lasting organizational change. This task requires an understanding of the issues of change (power, anxiety, and control) as well as an appreciation of what it takes to effectively initiate and manage change. Implementing reorientations is fundamentally different and more challenging than implementing incremental change. Whereas executive leadership can delegate incremental change, they must be directly involved in shaping and managing metamorphic change.

**Personally acting as an instrument.** Finally, the leader needs to be able to act effectively as an instrument. The executive must be able to share the strategic vision and make it real for people in the organization, to provide a sense of urgency about the need to change, to provide a context for designing the new organization, and to provide leadership in managing change. He or she must be able to articulate the vision, to energize people to work toward that vision, and to support behavior consistent with the strategic change.

## SUMMARY

In this final chapter, we have reflected on the key themes of this book, noted the limitations of design as a managerial tool, and placed design in the context of the strategic changes that organizations must make at different points in their development if they are to survive and prosper. Design is ultimately a part of the leader's job. While others may be called on to participate in designing, to react to designs, to provide suggestions, to do analysis, or to help in planning implementation, it is ultimately the leader's job to actively shape his or her organization. To ignore design is to throw away a potentially powerful tool for building effective organizations over time.

# Name Index

# Subject Index